IRISH STEAM IN THE 1960s

END OF AN ERA

A Personal Photographic Record

CONRAD NATZIO

COLOURPOINT

Published 2017 by Colourpoint Books
an imprint of Colourpoint Creative Ltd
Colourpoint House, Jubilee Business Park
21 Jubilee Road, Newtownards, BT23 4YH
Tel: 028 9182 6339
Fax: 028 9182 1900
E-mail: sales@colourpoint.co.uk
Web: www.colourpoint.co.uk

First Edition
First Impression

Text © Conrad Natzio, 2017
Illustrations © Conrad Natzio, 2017

A catalogue record for this book is available from the British Library.

Designed by April Sky Design, Newtownards
Tel: 028 9182 7195
Web: www.aprilsky.co.uk

Printed by GPS Colour Graphics Ltd, Belfast

ISBN 978-1-78073-146-9

Front cover: On a crisp February morning in 1961, 'VS' No 207, *Boyne*, leaves Amiens Street (now Connolly) Station with the 08.45 Thursdays-only 'shoppers' excursion to Belfast. This train ran all the year round, remained steam-hauled to the end, and was provided with the best available engine from Dublin shed.

Rear cover: On the line between Derriaghy and Lambeg, 'S' Slieve Donard passes McGredy's Rose Garden on an 'up' local (outward from Belfast) on 29 September 1962. I remember 'Mrs Sam McGredy' as a rose variety popular with gardeners in my parents' time, no doubt conceived in these now-vanished gardens.

About the author:
The author, a native of Cheshire, counts himself lucky to have arrived in Dublin as a student in October 1958, incidentally three weeks after the demise of the Great Northern Railway. Adding photography to his already well-developed interest in locomotives and their performance, he was able to witness and record the closing days of steam in Ireland. He was an early member of the Railway Preservation Society of Ireland, and regrets that his present domicile in Suffolk precludes more active membership; he hopes that contributing any royalties from this book to the RPSI might be a slight compensation.

CONTENTS

An October day in 1961 and 'J9' No 250 with a beet special takes the single line to Youghal, at Cobh Junction. Youghal still enjoyed a sketchy passenger service, lost in 1963 but now restored as far as Midleton for Cork commuters. Not unusually, a couple of covered wagons for general goods have been cut into the beet special.

List of Abbreviations

B&CDR: Belfast and County Down Railway; nationalised as part of UTA from 1949

B&NCR: Belfast and Northern Counties Railway, forerunner of the NCC

CIÉ: Córas Iompair Éireann (Irish Transport Company), nationalised universal transport system established in Southern Ireland in 1945

DDR: Dublin and Drogheda Railway

D&K: Dublin and Kingstown Railway, the first in Ireland, linking Dublin with Kingstown/ Dun Laoghaire

DN&GR: Dundalk Newry and Greenore Railway, cross-Border and owned by the (English) London & North Western Railway

D&SER: Dublin and South-Eastern Railway, formerly Dublin Wicklow & Wexford, incorporated into the GSR in 1925

F&RR&HC: Fishguard and Rosslare Railways and Harbours Company, ferry operators between points named; owned some connecting line(s) in Ireland

GNR(I), GNR, GN: Great Northern Railway (Ireland), international cross-Border system divided in 1958 between CIÉ and UTA

GS&WR, GSW: Great Southern and Western Railway, major company serving southern Ireland; largest constituent of GSR at 1924/5 amalgamation

GSR: Great Southern Railway, the 1924/5 amalgamation of all railway companies working entirely south of the Border (ie excluding GNR(I) and some others)

IRRS: Irish Railway Record Society, railway enthusiasts' association

MGWR: Midland Great Western Railway, serving western Ireland – part of GSR from 1924

NCC: Northern Counties Committee of the (English) Midland Railway, subsequently London Midland & Scottish; took over B&NCR in 1903, incorporated in nationalised UTA (q.v.) in 1949

RPSI: Railway Preservation Society of Ireland, cross-Border organisation mainly concerned with preserving and running rolling-stock

SL&NCR: Sligo Leitrim and Northern Counties Railway, notoriously impecunious cross-Border line between Enniskillen and Sligo, closed 1957

UTA: Ulster Transport Authority, nationalised (in 1949) amalgamation of all Northern Ireland transport systems

WL&WRC: Waterford Limerick and Western Railway Company, absorbed by G&SWR in 1901

INTRODUCTION

As those who lived through it will remember, the mid-20th century was a time of great social and technological change. A hundred years earlier the advent of the steam railway had brought its own social revolution, with the arrival of the age of mobility for the general public. But by the 1960s the next revolution in mass transport had taken place, in the shape of both the private car and the motor lorry. The railways were no longer a source of profit, but a liability to their owners who, in western Europe, had generally become the State. In some quarters the future of steel-wheel-on-steel-rail for the conveyance of passengers was already starting to be questioned. As for the – perhaps lovable, but increasingly demanding and uneconomic – steam locomotive, the writing on the wall was legible to all. Railway administrations were scrambling for a viable substitute, inevitably in the form of diesel traction, sometimes as a stopgap when ultimate electrification could be envisaged.

By comparison with their cross-channel counterparts the railways of Ireland were early into the field, both with diesel-mechanical railcars and diesel-electric locomotives. That steam traction should have survived at all by 1960, and indeed for a considerable time thereafter was, if not accidental, certainly not welcomed and least of all intended, by the managements of the two national rail authorities, Córas Iompair Éireann (CIÉ) in the South and the Ulster Transport Authority (UTA) in the North.

In the Republic, the initial dieselisation programme of CIÉ had been completed some years earlier, first with railcars taking over many passenger services and then with the delivery of the Sulzer and Metrovick/Crossley locomotives (the latter of somewhat doubtful reliability, not unwelcome to the steam enthusiast). In the North, the demise of UTA steam and its replacement by multi-purpose railcars had been predicted, with misplaced confidence, to be completed by 1960. But the final extinction and division in 1958 of the Great Northern Railway of Ireland (GNR(I), also GNR or GN) – by then of course the GNR Board, that remarkable internationalised concern – between the other two main players meant that they inherited a very mixed bag of locomotive assets. The precarious finances of the Great Northern left it far short of a complete modernisation of its motive power despite its early entry into the field of diesel traction. In May 1959 there had been a major transfer of diesel locomotives from CIÉ's own resources to their ex-GN lines; in the North, former Northern Counties Committee (NCC) steam locomotives started to appear on the UTA section, and supplemented but by no means entirely displaced the native stock.

It might come as a surprise, then, that a survey (unofficial, but well-informed) as late as the summer of 1962 should reveal that at least 159 steam locomotives had been active in Ireland during the previous twelve months. Of these, 105 were owned by CIÉ, of which 71, of no fewer than 19 different classes, originated with the Great Southern

Railways (or that company's constituents) while the other 34, of 15 classes, were inherited from the GNR. The UTA had 54, 25 being ex-NCC (3 classes), 27 ex-Great Northern (11 classes), plus two surviving 0-6-4Ts of the Sligo, Leitrim & Northern Counties Railway (SL&NCR). There was an extensive and varied collection, then, of idiosyncratic and often elusive engines for the enthusiast to seek out, photograph, and travel behind.

I had arrived in the autumn of 1958 as a callow undergraduate at Trinity College Dublin (TCD), without experience of the railways of Ireland apart from a childhood memory of a visit to the seaside at Greystones where I dimly recall black engines of unfamiliar appearance, visible from the beach, engaged in shunting coaches that even to my juvenile eyes had an antique look. In the spring of 1963, after TCD, and coincidentally with the definitive end of steam on CIÉ, I returned, as did so many others, to the other side of the water in search of gainful employment. Subsequent visits to the country were inevitably (so far as railway interest was concerned) to the North, where of course steam activity persisted for a few years longer.

The first two years at Trinity were spent, apart from occasional study, in exploration of the railway, and particularly locomotive, scene; in photographing the latter, at that stage in black-and-white; in monitoring with a stopwatch the performance of (mostly) ex-Great Northern engines which had been acquired by their new owners a few weeks before I first set eyes on them; and more important, in making friendships which were to prove lasting. These were initially among contemporaries whose names appear below, but I was lucky later on to get to know others of an older generation, notably RN (Bob) Clements, RM (Mac) Arnold, and Drew Donaldson. Not all the senior members of the enthusiast community were best known for suffering fools gladly, and that they seemed prepared to do so was something of a boost to my youthful self-confidence.

Fifty or sixty years ago, one 'came of age' at 21, and the relevance of this otherwise unremarkable event was the acquisition of both a decent camera and a decidedly second-hand black Morris Minor van. This handy and hardy vehicle opened up the prospects of lineside photography outside the immediate Dublin area. It later saw service much further afield, notably in the Peloponnese where metre-gauge 2-8-2s continued to roam, and – by then on its second replacement engine – in Normandy, in search of the venerable French Pacifics still in command on front-line duties. It may be remembered that in the Republic of the early sixties, neither driving tests nor speed limits existed to inconvenience the chasers of steam trains. In retrospect the van's regular crew, which generally included Norman Foster, David Houston, and Eddie Lewis, were perhaps lucky to survive unscathed, the former two both to gain respectability much later as Chairmen of the Railway Preservation Society of Ireland (RPSI). Among many recollections of the expeditions of those years, one is that of a return from Belfast late one night. The van had a very full crew of five, including Drew Donaldson *and his bicycle*. At the Southern Customs post it occurred to an officer, unusually, to open the back doors and inspect the inside – an idea quickly abandoned at the sight of the row of faces (and bike) in the light of his torch.

A not untypical scenario from the time! When pursuing a train from Vernersbridge (on the GN's Derry line) towards Belfast, it seemed from the map that use of the road ferry at Bannfoot might enable us to overtake it while it stopped at Portadown and Lurgan. Alas, this plan did not survive the first glimpse of the ferry's technology. Anyway, this is the vehicle which made many of these photographs possible, KYI 680, about to be driven off the ferry by Norman Foster.

Perhaps that incident is a reminder that the temper of those times was in some respects illusory. There seemed some prospect that the old political animosities were dying down; the grim decades to come were unforeseen. It was for instance possible to scramble about the fields around Bessbrook in search of a better viewpoint for Craigmore viaduct, without risking a misunderstanding of a particularly regrettable kind. The dark years that happened to follow the final demise of steam in Northern Ireland were lightened for some by the extraordinary resilience of the RPSI, initially operating from its Whitehead base, but from the outset a cross-Border institution committed to the running of steam trains in both North and South, with, it should be said, exemplary support from the two national rail authorities. To contribute any proceeds from the sale of this book to the Society will be at least a token recognition of the pleasure its activities have given to its members, and to the thousands of the general public, over the fifty and more years since its foundation.

By 1960, to photograph, and if possible record the performance, of steam locomotives required a good deal of time, travel, and patience. To find steam-hauled passenger trains it was usually necessary to go northwards from Dublin, where ex-Great Northern motive power from both new owners survived on former GN metals, with an injection of NCC types on remaining steam rosters on the UTA-owned section and on specials to Dublin and the South. On the NCC section itself, there were a few year-round steam turns on the Larne line, and plenty of summer workings to Portrush and Derry. Travel behind former Great Southern (GSR) engines, on the other hand, usually meant a long haul to one of the very few remaining steam-worked branches in the west, perhaps a very short trip on a boat train to Dun Laoghaire, or hitching a lift on a goods train. Certainly, the conversion of most locomotive working on the now CIÉ-owned Great Northern section to diesel haulage from existing resources did result in some steam substitution elsewhere on the system, to cover shortage or failures of the Metrovick engines, but the grapevine could not always predict when and where these would occur. Passenger engines of GSR origin were in any case of hen's teeth rarity by 1960. Yes, a very few Midland Great Western (MGW) 2-4-0s were still active; a single Great Southern and Western (GS&W) 4-4-0 was resurrected, to general surprise, from the back of Limerick shed to work through flood waters impassible to railcars; and Dubliners were given to understand that one or two 4-6-0 monsters still shambled round the yards of Cork, occasionally to be let out to work an overload goods to Mallow or Thurles. But lineside photography on the former GSR network usually involved 0-6-0s on ballast trains or seasonal beet workings, a disillusioned approach to the working timetable, a trust that optimism about the weather would be justified, and a resignation to long and sometimes disappointing waits for that distant plume of steam, often followed by a more or less hectic pursuit over questionable rural roads. It will become apparent that my interest was, and is, in what the locomotives were doing, and how they and their trains looked when they were doing it.

The information accompanying these photographs (which are neither chronological nor comprehensive) comes partly from personal observation and conversation, but a list of printed sources also appears at the end. I owe a huge debt to those whose names appear above, and to others unnamed, not least to those railwaymen who in the 1960s were continuing to maintain a public service, often in working conditions little changed over the previous century. For those too young to remember those times, I hope that these pictures may convey some suggestion of a way of life and work, as well sometimes of a landscape, now lost for ever – and that they will stir memories for those who were there. The photographs are grouped loosely by subject matter, with a short introduction to each section.

Conrad Natzio
October 2017

The Great Northern Main Line

The author's partiality for the Great Northern – I once heard it described by a Dublin enthusiast as "a proper railway", evidently in unflattering comparison with some other lines – will become apparent. The sight of a 'VS' No 209, *Foyle*, leaving Amiens Street (as it then was) station on my second day in Dublin was enough to ignite the fires of this long-lasting affair. *Foyle* did not last long after that day in October 1958; neither did her sister No 206, *Liffey*, but CIÉ's inheritance still included enough passenger engines to cover all remaining requirements after the diesels arrived the following May. In fact, by the start of the period covered by this book, there was only one all-the-year-round passenger turn for steam – a morning and evening commuter service to Howth – and scheduled goods workings were headed by the invasive 'A' Class diesels. Nevertheless the demands of summer traffic, diesel unreliability, and special working provided many, if often unpredictable, opportunities for photography and travel, for those who could be in the right place at the right time.

Where else but Amiens Street (now Connolly) Station to start a tour of the Great Northern? On a crisp February morning in 1961, 'VS' No 207, *Boyne*, leaves with Driver Hughie Penrose in charge, with the 08.45 Thursdays-only 'shoppers' excursion to Belfast. This train ran all the year round, remained steam-hauled to the end, and was provided with the best available engine from Dublin shed. The sole surviving compound, No 85 *Merlin*, was used from early 1959 (when she emerged from overhaul at Dundalk Works) until 207 was similarly outshopped in May the following year. The 08.45 ran non-stop in the down direction, and also on the return until one evening Micky Boyce, with little experience of this working, caused considerable embarrassment to the Customs by running into Dublin unusually early. Thereafter a stop was made at Dundalk to pick up the officers, and most drivers took the opportunity to put some water in the tender tank. The return train in particular was subject to delays north of the Border, and water could cause some anxiety when the load rose to the normal maximum of 10 bogies. The 08.45 was my own favoured magic carpet, sometimes possible even in term time, and I see that, with 85 and 207, I clocked up over 7500 miles on these trains alone. If neither big engine was available, one of the three 'S' class had to be used, and I recorded non-stop runs with all three – 170 (*Errigal*), 171 (*Slieve Gullion*), and 174 (*Carrantuohill*). The last-named

(again with Penrose and Fireman Mick Welsh) achieved the run almost at the eleventh hour for steam, on the 29 November 1962, in a net time only four minutes outside the 135-minute booking of the 'Enterprise', and with a 7-coach load.

Ex-NCC locomotives began to infiltrate the former GN line soon after the system was divided, and reached Dublin quite often on specials and when railcars were unable to cope with the traffic. Belfast ran its own Thursday 'Tourist Train' to Dublin in summer, returning in a path from Amiens Street at 18.20. Usually one of the two 'VS's (*Lagan* and *Erne*, formerly 208 and 210 but now renumbered 58 and 59) appeared, but 'Moguls' might be used as necessary. Here it is No 94, *The Maine*, departing with the 18.20; she was one of the less frequent visitors, but with her I recorded my fastest-ever run with steam on the GN, with Belfast's Billy Bateson and 6 bogies, passing Dundalk South in 22'36" for the 22.0 miles from the Drogheda start and touching 78 mph in the process, before being stopped by signal outside the station. This was on 18 March 1963, with what Drew Donaldson used to call the 'Dog-men's Train', a special returning Northern visitors and others from the regular Dublin dog show on the St Patrick's Day Bank Holiday.

Three-quarters of a mile out of Amiens Street, the line crosses the Tolka Bridge, reconstructed after the original was destroyed in the floods of December 1954. During the work passenger trains terminated at Clontarf, and freight ran via Drogheda, Navan, and the former Midland & Great Western branch to Dublin. A 'Glover tank' ('T2' 4-4-2 No 143) is crossing with the morning steam commuter service from Howth; in the background is East Wall signal cabin, controlling the junction on the up side with the North Wall Extension and yards.

Here *Carrantuohill* is heading the evening 17.50 trip to Howth on the 'Stone Arch' across the Clontarf Road, in April 1961. Sharp-eyed readers may notice that the leading coach is in UTA Brunswick green; this is indeed a UTA set, marooned in Dublin by IRA activity at the Border which even in the relatively peaceful 1960s sometimes caused disruption. It looks as if Amiens Street staff decided to use this set to get it out of the way at a busy time of the evening.

A few hundred yards further north, close to the site of the former Clontarf station, is a surviving structure of the Dublin and Drogheda Railway (DDR), the Howth Road bridge. The DDR's name is perpetuated on a cast iron plate on the arch. The 18.20 return special to Belfast on 10 August 1961 is headed by *Erne*, renumbered 59 in the UTA list and without her GN insignia. Her driver from Belfast (Adelaide) shed looks like, indeed surely is, Arthur Boreland, a frequent visitor to Dublin on these trains, not least because he never converted to modern traction.

Immediately after Malahide station the main line crosses the Broadmeadow estuary, the first of two tidal inlets, by a mile-long embankment interrupted by a 600-foot viaduct. The original timber bridge was replaced in 1860 by wrought-iron girders; these were strengthened about 1930, but by the time CIÉ took over these were in an unimpressive state, and an irregularly observed speed limit of 50 mph was imposed. A prestressed concrete structure was installed in 1968, and lasted until August 2009, when the driver of an up train managed to get clear and into Malahide station to give the alarm, having seen the bridge starting to give way in front of him. The scouring effect of the ebb tide is apparent in this view of *Erne*, with an up special for a Rugby International match, on a rough 11 February 1961. The driver on this occasion was Adelaide's Ralph McBrien, who gave enthusiasts many enjoyably brisk performances.

Here the returning 'Tourist' is running off the northern end of the embankment behind 59 again, on a more peaceful May evening in 1961. The short sixth vehicle is one of the GN's two kitchen cars, this being No 399, taken into UTA stock at the division of the spoils. Arthur Boreland has no doubt eased *Erne* scrupulously over the bridge, and has now applied steam to get up the gentle rise to Donabate.

Photos of *Merlin* are unfortunately rare in this collection, the reason being that whenever possible I tried to be in her train rather than watching it. Happily this omission can be remedied in the twenty-first century, now that she is enjoying a longer career in preservation than she did in company service. However, here she is "shovelling white steam over her shoulder" (WH Auden's 'Night Mail') with the 08.45 on the embankment across the Rogerstown estuary, the second of the two, between Donabate and Rush, in October 1960. The driver, Dublin's Jerry Whelan, might perhaps have regretted the absence of smoke deflectors, if the wind had not been westerly…

…or maybe not: it's hard to believe that Hughie Penrose, working the same train with 207 a year later, could have had much view of where he was going. Possibly the taller deflectors fitted on 206 and 209 would have been more effective. The location is the site of the short-lived Baldoyle station, open for a couple of years in the 1840s before the Howth branch was completed. Howth Junction is less than a mile to the south, and recent building development makes this rural scene unimaginable today.

Summer evening at Rogerstown, and a first, if distant, glimpse of one of the two 'Q' class engines which CIÉ were fortunate to inherit, both at the time being fresh from a Dundalk overhaul (No 131) or still in the shops (No 132, seen here). Both ran many useful miles for their new owners; for a few months at the end of 1958/early 1959 there was a motive power shortage, and this pair were to be found once again taking expresses out of Dublin, the work for which the class was introduced in 1899. It was behind 131, driven by Tommy Rooney of Dundalk on the 14.30 from Dublin, that I recorded a speed

of 77 mph down the gentle descent to Laytown in March 1959. Here 132 is more modestly in charge of the 18.35 Dublin–Skerries and return, often steam-worked in the summer of 1961. This was a smartly-timed operation which saw the train back in Amiens Street 86 minutes after leaving; 13 intermediate stops had to be made in the course of the round trip of 35.8 miles, with 12 minutes allowed to run round the train at Skerries and depart from the down platform. No 132 could do it all right, but not with much to spare, running in the high 50s between stations even when tender-first.

Balbriggan was a favourite destination for weekend trippers from Dublin in high summer. The approach was over a long viaduct beside the harbour, and here an 'SG2' 0-6-0, probably No 184, is bringing in a seaside train – its nature apparent from the number of heads at the windows – on 24 June 1961. The engine will run round, take water, and return the empty carriages to Dublin for another load, and the returns could go on till quite late in the evening.

17

Balbriggan in winter: Paddy Rafferty brings *Merlin* into the station on a very mundane train, the Saturdays-only 13.25 Dublin–Drogheda local, on 9 December 1961. By this time coaches of CIÉ origin were making their appearance on the ex-GN system, and it can just be seen here that her train consists of a set of the 1956 lightweight stock with unpainted aluminium alloy finish.

Between Balbriggan and Drogheda the line crosses two minor rivers, at Gormanston and Laytown, by short viaducts. This is the first, and No 197 *Lough Neagh* (one of the very pretty 'U' class of 1915) is crossing with a down train on 24 June 1961. This looks like a seaside train which has discharged its passengers at Balbriggan, to judge by (a) the open windows and (b) the absence of occupants, and is running on to Drogheda to stable the stock. Connoisseurs of such matters might take a second look at 197's tender, which looks much like one of those supplied by Beyer Peacock with the second batch of 'U's in 1948. In fact, it is one of the seven built new as late as 1955/6 for use with existing engines, of which five came from Beyers, but two, of

which this was one (identifiable by the lack of access cut-outs in the frames), were built at Dundalk. Insofar as a tender can be regarded as part of a locomotive, they might be said to be the last locomotive products of that famous works.

Later that day No 99 *Lough Derg,* a 1915 sister to *Lough Neagh,* crosses the same viaduct on a similar working. She is in virtually original condition, with flush-headed rivets on the smokebox, apart from her livery and name – and the smokebox door fitting, with a locking handwheel substituted for the second, outer, handle. Presumably it was found that the outer handle worked loose under its own weight if in the left-hand quadrant. The changed arrangement seems to have appeared first on the GNR with the 'SG3' 0-6-0s when new in 1921, and to have been generally adopted thereafter. The same change took place on the GSR over the same period, and all Irish engines thereafter took on a characteristic 'face'. Oddly enough it was the double handle which became the usual, though not universal, standard on the railways of Britain.

We are at Drogheda, on 28 April 1961, and *Errigal* shows off the glories of the full GNR blue livery. Having been overhauled at Dundalk in 1959 under CIÉ auspices she is however without GN lettering or crest. She has brought in the Saturday 13.25 and has visited the shed to be turned. To keep the rather tight 60 minute booking for the 31.7 miles (including eight stops) with a minute to spare, Jack Traynor has had to do some 60 mph running between stops with his 5 coach train.

Sitting in Drogheda's up bay platform is everyone's favourite engine (mine, at any rate) – at the time of writing, No 131 is about to return to the main line after a chequered history since her withdrawal in 1963. On 14 April 1962 she looks all of her 61 years of age, nearly four years after her last general repair, and has acquired an ill-matched F-type tender. Nevertheless she has just been doing 65 mph down from Kellystown, on a rather odd working. At this period no diesel locomotive could be found for the 12.45 up stopping train from Dundalk, so it was the practice to use the Dundalk passenger pilot as far as Drogheda, where an 'A' Class was on hand to take over.

Drogheda's locomotive depot usually held a small and undistinguished resident allocation. However, the shed's annual big day was the Sunday in May when the commemoration of the Blessed Oliver

Plunkett brought pilgrims from the North by special train. On this damp morning in 1962, the visitors arrived behind a 'VS', No 59 *Erne*, and two NCC 'Moguls', Nos 98 and 99. Perhaps it was a sign of the apparently more settled political times that, for this of all occasions, Belfast had no inhibitions about turning out the two 'Moguls' named after British monarchs, *Edward VIII* and *George VI* respectively. It may be remembered that for the 1936 NCC/GNR locomotive exchange, it was thought prudent to remove the nameplates of No 96, *Silver Jubilee*, before she was sent to Dublin.

Arthur Boreland has backed 98 on to the turntable, and his fireman is applying muscle power, supervised by Norman Foster. No 98 is in an interestingly hybrid condition; she was the only 'Mogul' to retain an original Fowler-pattern chimney, was one of the only two (with 104) to acquire outside steampipes, and had been turned out from her last overhaul in 1961 with her original small tender – soon replaced however as seen here with a 3500-gallon version from the withdrawn 96. The NCC duplicated the engine's numberplate on the back of the tender. I wonder, but never thought to check, if the plates were changed when tenders were swapped in later years? Note, in the background, the remarkable resemblance between the 3500-gallon Stanier tender of 99 and the Great Northern 4000-gallon F-type of No 59.

The Boyne Bridge at Drogheda and Craigmore Viaduct at Bessbrook could compete for the title of 'Most Spectacular Engineering Work' on the GN main line. This view of the former looks northward on the afternoon of 16 December 1961. The only survivor of the five 'QNG' class 0-6-0s of 1911, No 112, is not about to overrun a stop signal; she is *propelling* her train on to the gauntletted tracks on the bridge, and after crossing will continue on the *up* line until reaching the facing junction to the marshalling yard and branch down to the cement factory at river level. In the distance a plume of steam can just be made out, and this comes from No 131, safely away on the down line and returning light to Dundalk after the working described above. No 112 was a long-term Drogheda resident, and her high tractive effort thanks to her small wheels (4'7¼" as opposed to the 5'1" of later GN goods engines) was no doubt helpful in getting loaded trains up the steep climb from the river.

After crossing the Boyne, down trains have a four-mile climb to the summit at milepost 37¼, marked by Kellystown signal cabin, reputedly the smallest in Ireland. The only function of this box was to divide the 10-mile section from Drogheda to Dunleer, and it was switched out except at particularly busy times. Here the daily goods from Ardee tops the five-mile bank southbound from Dunleer behind 'SG2' No 15, and passes the box on a soft winter's day in December 1961.

On the same morning, No 15 is starting her train away from the junction with the Ardee branch at Dromin. The station here was finally closed to passengers in 1955, but the branch itself had lost its service in 1934.

23

Dromiskin level crossing marks the foot of the 12-mile racing stretch northwards from Kellystown. Speeds of 70-plus could be expected, though I never recorded more than 79 – very properly, no doubt, in view of the nominal restriction to 70. Here *Boyne*, under new management having been sold to the UTA after the end of steam on CIÉ, is wheeling the 'Tourist' train homeward on a July evening in 1964.

This is Dundalk, and No 131 is standing in the down platform with the above-mentioned 12.45 *up* train on 14 April 1962. Dundalk was of course a Customs station, and the up platform was fenced off and gated. Passengers for trains which had come across the Border were obliged to wait while the train was supposedly rummaged, seldom in my experience with profitable results. On busy days the queue might stretch back up the ramp towards the station entrance at street level.

By the summer of 1963 the NCC 2-6-4 tanks (the 'Jeeps') were a familiar, indeed the usual, power on passenger services north of Dundalk, though 'Moguls' also appeared. Here No 56, of the final batch built in 1950 – the last main-line steam locomotives built for an Irish railway – has taken over the 18.30 express from Dublin from the green-painted 'A' Class diesel to be seen lurking outside the former paint shop; the engine has been turned at Dundalk shed after working an up service, but the crew are topping up with water from the familiar balloon tank. The 'Jeeps' were in principle well suited to most of the passenger services on the former Great Northern, and coped effectively for the years to 1965, after some early difficulties for their crews caused by both the different firing technique and the unfamiliar steam brake.

By 1960, the importance of Dundalk as a railway centre was greatly diminished. The 'Irish North', the network serving the hinterland between the CIÉ-served Midlands and the GN's 'Derry Road', had disappeared following the Government-imposed closure of the parts in the North and the consequent loss, delayed for a couple of years, of the southern remnants. The Greenore line – that anomalous outpost of the London & North Western Railway – had gone in 1952. The stub to Barrack Street survived until 1995, the sole relic of the old Irish North Western, and here the last of the 'QG' 0-6-0s of 1904, No 155, is doing some shunting. These were the goods version of the 'Q's, and their low-pitched boiler perhaps gives some idea of how the latter looked before their rebuilding with superheaters and piston valves in the 1920s.

Immediately after leaving Dundalk, the line crosses the Castletown river. By April 1962 the reign of the 'Jeeps' on the GN was well-established, including

their use on goods trains. They were just as strong as the Moguls (though less so than a GN 'SG3' 0-6-0 in power class 'D'), but controlling a loose-coupled freight was tricky without the extra braking power of a tender. This unidentified engine has a moderate load and is managing without rear-end assistance.

Serious climbing starts a little further on, at about milepost 56, for six miles at 1 in 100 or a little easier to Adavoyle station, where a short dip gives some impetus for the final couple of miles to the summit at mp 65¼. The challenge to down trains posed by the Carlingford mountains in the background is obvious in this shot of No 55, running downhill to Dundalk with the 18.15 Belfast–Dublin express on an August evening in 1963. The square white board by the down line marks a catch point, that very desirable safeguard against breakaways.

It's February 1961, and snow is still lying on Slieve Gullion, visible ahead as the 14.45 from Dublin climbs the last couple of hundred yards to the Border, near mp 59½. However, it is not *Slieve Gullion* in charge but 'Jeep' No 51, and speed is unhappily down to less than 20 mph. Bob Perry of Portadown and his mate are having the struggle experienced by a good many GN crews in the early days of the influx of NCC engines. It is reported that the NCC firemen too had at first found the tanks less free steaming than their 'Moguls'. There were regrettable cases of engines stalling on the climb to Adavoyle for lack of steam. I came to a stand only once, and behind a 'Mogul' (No 98) at that, though Sam Heasley of the Adelaide top link did have the excuse of an unusually heavy train, ten bogies and a van, perhaps 350 tons full. Speed had not fallen below 22 mph when steam was shut off, so I suspect low water level rather than steaming was the problem. So 98 came off at Portadown, and the crew took over a trusty 'S', No 60 ex-172 *Slieve Donard,* and with this big train actually picked up a couple of minutes of the lost time.

This lineside photo shows an unusually lightly loaded 'Tourist' behind *Boyne*, climbing the big bank at exactly the same spot as the previous shot, but three years later, on an August evening in 1964. Though the gradient has eased slightly from the steepest pitch (the two miles at 1 in 91/100 past Mount Pleasant), the curvature and wet cuttings could still cause problems with slipping on the upper stretches of the ascent to Adavoyle with a heavy train. There were 388 feet to climb in the eleven miles between Dundalk and the final summit near milepost 65½.

We are now over the top, and a first sight of a 'Big D', an 'SG3' – the largest 0-6-0 in Ireland – earning its keep in heavy freight haulage. This is No 33, formerly 20, now renumbered by the UTA. She still looks in decent condition in the summer of 1963, having been given an overhaul in York Road shops in 1960, and is not making unduly heavy weather of the long grind on the 1 in 111 southbound to the summit. She has acquired one of the 1956 2500-gallon tenders in place of the flush-sided 3500-gallon type which she had from new in 1921.

An unidentifiable 'Jeep' has just topped the bank with a northbound goods, on a damp December day in 1961. She is still steaming, no doubt to keep couplings taut, and the white plume in the distance suggests that she has a banker in rear…

…as indeed proves to be the case; an 'SG3' from Dundalk has provided assistance up the hill, and by remaining coupled on the descent to Goraghwood is still useful in view of the difficulty the tank engine might have in braking a heavy load on a steep bank. Note that train engine and banker, and their crews, are of different nationalities, though the latter would no doubt regard themselves all as Great Northern men! In sight in the distance is Cloghogue Chapel ('Father Murphys'), always a welcome sight to crews – the firemen in particular – of up trains.

Immediately beyond Bessbrook station (closed in 1942, but rebuilt and reopened in 1984 as 'Newry', nine years after that town, now city, had lost its own railway) is Craigmore viaduct, on a right-hand curve and down gradient of 1 in 150. Pre-war trains often ran fast over the viaduct. It was surely one of the spots which Bob Clements had in mind, in writing that the accelerated timings of 1932 could only be kept "with speeds higher than were advisable on certain parts of the road", and a 50 mph limit was subsequently imposed. To feel oneself apparently launched into space on this curve at 50 was an agreeable sensation; at 60 there might be a slight *frisson*; at 70-plus, latterly a rare enough event, one might well agree with Bob. With other members of the RPSI I once had this experience behind a perhaps deceptively smooth-riding 'Jeep', No 56, which held the rails at 76 mph. In this shot, 'Mogul' No 97 (*Earl of Ulster*) is running the regular Sunday 18.00 Dublin–Belfast sedately downhill in the evening sunshine. This train remained booked for steam as late as 1964, to give more accommodation than the UTA railcars could provide. The Bessbrook and Newry Tramway ran beneath the viaduct, in the valley in the foreground, from 1885 to 1948.

Sunday 24 September 1961, a fine autumn day, saw Down play and duly beat Offaly in the All-Ireland Senior Football final at Dublin's Croke Park, watched by a record crowd of 90,500. A good many of the Down supporters travelled in six special trains, all steam-hauled, as also was the strengthened ordinary service train. This was probably the last such turn-out on the Great Northern main line, though alas, the motive power consisted, with one exception, of NCC types. The first three specials passed the Adavoyle area in the grey light of early morning with two 'Jeeps' and 'Mogul' No 98, the latter bearing a headboard with the message, momentarily confusing to the railway-minded, 'Up Down'. Adelaide shed had provided a galaxy of driving talent, for next (seen here) there came out of the morning mists No 93, *The Foyle* (still with her original small tender) with Arthur Boreland in charge, followed by Ned O'Hara on No 104 and lastly Billy Bateson on *Lagan*. George Ferguson had No 99 on the service train, which the photographers boarded at Goraghwood.

All the 'Moguls' had on this occasion to cope with 10-coach trains. No 104 is here seen on Craigmore viaduct – she was no engineman's favourite, but performed creditably that day with O'Hara. We travelled on their return train, which stopped at Goraghwood, and she both climbed and ran well, reaching 76 mph on the descent from Kellystown.

The last of the three specials was headed by the only GN representative, *Lagan,* and with Billy Bateson she looks to be going strongly on the Dublin Road bridge, close by 'Father Murphys'. This last train perhaps enjoyed (if only because of the engine!) somewhat higher status than its predecessors – what can be seen of the rolling stock looks rather more prepossessing than that of the earlier trains. The leading coach looks like an ex-NCC third brake, which suggests that the net had to be cast quite wide to find enough stock for the day.

A decidedly grubby tank coasts down past Mullaghglass on the approach to Goraghwood in August 1963. The train is the 09.15 from Dublin, by that period commonly made up of modern CIÉ stock, certainly more comfortable for second class passengers than the grim open 'thirds', which the GN continued to build until 1932. They had wooden bodies, often bare boards on the floor, and seated five abreast with a narrow centre aisle. On an early journey I was interested to see the window beside me working in its frame as speed rose into the sixties.

'Jeep' 55 gets away from the 'Wood' with the 15.15 goods from Portadown to Dundalk, allowed two hours for the 33¼ miles, including a 20-minute stop at Goraghwood to allow HM Customs to clear the train and the engine to take a drink. Down goods trains paused for a much longer inspection; the examination for passengers on the other hand verged on the perfunctory, completed on some trains in no more than ten minutes. The line from Warrenpoint and Newry ran up to join the main line at the station, and the branch outer home signal for Goraghwood can be seen on the right of the engine.

Steaming up the bank on the last few yards into Goraghwood with the (vintage) Warrenpoint branch train comes the very last GN 'PP' class 4-4-0 to survive, No 74. The number on the buffer beam can be disregarded; the famously independent-minded shed staff at Newry had no doubt that this engine was in better shape than the original No 42, also in their care, and when 74 was summoned for scrapping it was a simple paint job to swap identities and dispatch 42 to the scrapyard. 74 was in fact one of the oldest of the class, one of the first batch built in 1896. This photo is dated 8 August 1961, and the official withdrawal date was not until July 1963 – but I doubt if she had turned a wheel for some time before that.

35

A general view of Goraghwood on the afternoon of 19 March 1962. 'U' No 66 (ex-201) *Meath* of the second, 1948, batch has just arrived with the afternoon goods from the Warrenpoint branch. The 'Wood' was an important junction, and of course Customs point, and even if there were few local passengers there was brisk business with those changing trains from or to Newry and the 'Point'. Now there is nothing whatever left of the various installations, and it would take a very sharp-eyed passenger in a passing train to identify the site of Goraghwood station.

All trains stopped at the 'Wood', other than the 'Enterprise' and some specials. This is the up Sunday 09.30 Belfast–Dublin, booked for steam in the summer timetable (ie able to offer a ten coach train, rather than the eight of a full railcar set). On 12 August 1962 *Lagan* is ready to depart, with ten on, and no surprise by now that the driver should be Arthur Boreland.

The same train had reverted to steam on the Sunday of that All-Ireland final: this is No 99 entering Goraghwood with another ten coaches, and George Ferguson also did well – with this load, under 30 minutes from Dundalk to Drogheda was very fair going for a 'Mogul', before they ran unsurprisingly into signal checks. This shot seems to emphasise the relatively small size of the 'Mogul' boiler, perched above the wide running plates, and I sometimes thought that a stranger, walking up the platform to see what the engine was like, might get a first glimpse of a big Stanier tender and the side-window cab, and then be disappointed to find nothing bigger beyond. The train is passing the quarry (now long closed), with its crushing plant, which supplied the GN with ballast.

No 207 is here seen accelerating fast from the Goraghwood stop down into the dip at milepost 74, close to Knockarney crossing, once a request stop for railcars. By August 1963, with the end of steam on CIÉ, *Boyne* had been sold to the UTA along with the three 'S' class. All had been stripped of their nameplates, leaving an unpainted patch which was never touched up, except in 207's case, in which Adelaide shed took the trouble to fit a replacement wooden nameplate.

In this scene near Knockarney, perhaps not all is quite as it might at first glance appear. A close look reveals that the engine has been standing and dribbling on to the track for a while, and there is a light skim of rust on the rails in front of it. This is a Sunday morning, 20 August 1961, Newry shed has turned out 74/42 on a works train for reballasting on the up line, and wrong-line working is in force over the down, quite a serious matter with the summer Sunday excursions for Warrenpoint to come. Presumably 74 picked up her train at the Goraghwood quarry, rolled it down to Poyntzpass, ran round there and then worked forward to the work site.

In the summer of 1963, another grimy 'Jeep' brings an up express over the canal bridge between Knockarney and Poyntzpass. Few attempts at keeping locomotives clean were being made by now except for special occasions. The Newry canal was notable as the first summit level canal (the level being between Poyntzpass and Scarva) to be constructed in these islands. It was opened in 1742, as a means of conveying coal from the Coalisland collieries to Dublin by sea from Newry. Ironically, as we shall see, coal was latterly imported from Britain and transhipped at Newry on to rail; the canal had long been disused when the abandonment order was made in 1954. During the brief life of the Ballinamore and Ballyconnell Canal, it would have been theoretically possible to travel by inland waterway from Newry, via Lough Neagh, to Belfast or Coleraine, or by the Ulster Canal and Upper Lough Erne and the Shannon, to Limerick or through the Grand Canal either to Dublin or by the River Barrow to Waterford.

Comings and goings at Scarva, in this case No 55 passing with the moderately-loaded 15.15 Portadown–Dundalk goods on 16 September 1961, were supervised by the stolid though not solid figure on the down platform. The reverse curves imposed an imperfectly-observed limit to 50 mph, raised to 70 in recent years; anything much above 60 could in fact feel quite exciting. Banbridge branch trains were served by a bay behind the up platform, until the branch succumbed in 1955 despite the use of railcars and railbuses capable of making roadside stops.

From 1842 to 1970, Portadown was served by a station (strictly, by two successive stations) on the east bank of the Bann. The current replacement, less architecturally distinguished, on the other side of the river is at least more convenient for the town centre. Here 'SG2' No 16, now renumbered 38 in the UTA list, crosses the Bann on a down goods, almost at the platform end of the old station.

Taking water at the up end of Portadown's No 2 platform on 2 March 1963 is No 62 *Lugnaquilla*, formerly 190, one of the three 'S2' locomotives of which two (Nos 190 and 192) were inherited by the UTA, given an overhaul at the former NCC shops at York Road, and repainted in the UTA lined black livery

which looked well when clean; she has one of the D2 type tenders with a high coping. The 'S2's were always said to be less lively than the original five 'S's, from which they differed only by the arrangement of the valve gear. My experience of the class was too limited to reach any conclusion, but some prewar records suggest that anything lacking in high speed achievement was compensated by uphill ability. In 1927 Cecil J Allen rode the very rough 191 from Belfast to Dundalk on the Mail with Driver Lisk on a dark and dirty night, having the same week footplated a 'King' from Paddington to Plymouth – some contrast! They touched 80 in the descent from Adavoyle – "a truly tempestuous descent… I rarely remember being so thoroughly thrilled on the footplate". No 62/190, an unlucky engine, was involved in two fatal accidents: in 1933 her train was derailed near Dromiskin during the bitter railway strike of that year (probably unintentionally, but it seems that warning detonators were ignored after a rail had been removed). In 1946 a broken connecting rod pierced the firebox, killing the driver and a locomotive inspector. She certainly gave me a nervous moment once during a run on the Derry Road, running down Carrickmore bank (significantly on 12 July?) with speed rising from 50 to 60 on the 30 mph-restricted reverse curves.

No 55 is standing at the south (or west) end of Portadown station with the 18.15 Belfast–Dublin express on 8 August 1961. My notes of this trip imply that the van behind the engine was added to the eight-coach train at Portadown, but this would suggest that 55 came off the train to collect it from No 3 platform, perhaps after it was detached from the up Derry Mail: a plausible manoeuvre, but not one I recall. Anyway, here is one of the last steam locomotives to be built for an Irish railway, replete with all the latest refinements that the LMS (or rather, British Railways, in their brief ownership of the NCC system in 1948/49) could provide while this batch of 'Jeeps' were under construction at Derby, including rocking grates, self-cleaning smokeboxes, and exhaust injectors. But coupled to the engine is none other than this Great Northern six-wheeled 'W' van, smartly repainted in CIÉ green, No 292, built in 1890! Incidentally, the load was made up at Dundalk from eight bogies and a van to thirteen and three vans, 430 tons full, the heaviest I ever knew on the GN; too heavy anyway for timekeeping with the 'A' class diesel which took over at Dundalk.

Stations came thick and fast in the last fifteen miles into Belfast, eleven in all – some, as at Damhead, classified as halts. *Erne* is passing with one of the Drogheda pilgrim trains on that Sunday morning in May 1962.

On 2 March 1963 Tommy Redpath of Adelaide is pausing with *Lugnaquilla* at Maze, another rather basic establishment, on a Saturday lunchtime local to Portadown. Even in March, the snows of the brutal winter of 1962/63 are still thick on the shaded side of the cutting. A few months later, on 4 August, Driver Redpath extracted from No 207 what appears to have been the highest power output recorded by a Great Northern locomotive, in maintaining 40 mph on the 1 in 100 section of the climb to Adavoyle with a nine-coach train of 295 tons, while working the summer Sunday 18.20 from Dublin. The same engine and load virtually repeated this effort on that train a year later.

Knockmore was the junction for both the GN line to Antrim (hidden by the train, going off to the right) and the Banbridge branch, closed in 1956 apart from a half-mile stub surviving as Newforge Siding, closed in the year of this photo, 1962. The junction points are visible, diverging from the up road on the left. 'Jeep' No 50 passes on a Portadown–Belfast local.

Lisburn was the terminus of many local services. Although only seven-and-a-half miles from Belfast's Great Victoria Street, there were, and are, seven intermediate stations, so that smart acceleration was a desirable attribute. Steam railmotors and push-and-pull trains provided none too successful competition with trams a century ago. By our period conventional steam trains could be hauled by any type of locomotive, up to the occasional 'VS'. In this shot taken on 2 March 1963, 'Mogul' 93, *The Foyle*, brings in a local for Portadown; by now this engine has acquired a big Stanier tender replacing the original. The headlamps look smart, repainted in NCC style, but the implied express status of the train can be disregarded. Water is still available for RPSI steam locomotives from the down platform tank.

We have now reached Belfast (Great Victoria Street) terminus, 112.6 miles from Dublin. The Boyne Bridge carries Durham Street across the station, and No 2 platform is barricaded off to inconvenience potential smugglers. Hughie Penrose and Mick Welsh are preparing to leave with *Boyne* on the 19.10 return excursion to Dublin, August Bank Holiday, 6 August 1962. Their load is nine bogies, but in the morning they had worked eleven down non-stop, an exceptional feat, running cautiously at the start and finish to conserve water, but from Drogheda to Goraghwood actually improved on the former 'Enterprise' timing. On the right is a coach newly and smartly repainted in UTA green, looking like a non-corridor first or first/second composite brake with a very small guard's compartment at the far end, perhaps G6 No 238 of 1931. The present station is very different from the one seen here, which was demolished in 1976, at the nadir of the railways' fortunes in Northern Ireland. The replacement 'Central' station was/is nothing of the sort, though at least bringing all lines serving Belfast under one roof. The proximity of Great Victoria Street to the city centre led to its reconstruction in 1995, and a brisk commuter traffic in consequence.

Great Northern branches

By 1960, of course, the GNR system had been drastically pruned. Going north from Dublin, Howth remained a busy commuter terminus. The long branch from Drogheda to Oldcastle via Navan only had a daily goods train (plus one to Kingscourt, by the ex-MGW line from Navan), as did Ardee. The entire 'Irish North' system, the lines west of Dundalk and south of Portadown–Derry, had been expunged from the map as a result of the Northern government's policies in 1957, the truncated remains south of the Border being unable to survive. Branches to Banbridge and Castlewellan/ Newcastle had gone already, and ominous noises relating to the Derry line itself were becoming audible, even though traffic, particularly in summer, appeared to be holding up well. Three buffet-car expresses a day still connected the Maiden City and intermediate points with Belfast. The Lisburn–Antrim line lost its passenger service on (as it happens) my 21st birthday in September 1960 and survived only as a link between the GN and NCC sections of the UTA. The populous town, now city, of Newry still had a reasonable service, extended sketchily to Warrenpoint all the year round, with a much enhanced timetable at summer weekends; but it was tolerably clear that the dominant road lobby had this branch in its sights also.

Most passenger services on the lines mentioned were operated by diesel railcars, but the diligent follower of steam could nevertheless build up a reasonably convincing portfolio. We'll deal briefly in the following pages with the Howth and Antrim branches, and at slightly greater length with the more atmospheric lines to Warrenpoint and Derry.

The single-platform terminus at Howth was pleasantly situated beside the harbour, and in earlier times the Great Northern issued combined travel and bathing tickets for use in its own shelters; presumably the building in the foreground is a later construction! The Howth tram, lost in 1959, terminated outside the station after a steep descent from the Hill, generally undertaken by gravity. The train is the 18.24 from Howth on a May evening in 1962, the return of the one rush-hour working still booked for steam, no doubt because of insufficient accommodation on the 4-coach AEC railcars generally used on the branch. The engine is one of the couple of 'T2' class 4-4-2Ts left in Dublin, No 3 not No 65, as suggested by the replacement front buffer beam from the withdrawn former owner, installed after a slight bump-up.

No 3 is restarting her train from Sutton, the only intermediate station on the branch. The tramway started (or finished) here, on the far side of the wall on the right; one of the tram poles has evidently survived since the closure, on 31 May 1959, and the house next to it is in characteristic Great Northern style – the stationmaster's, or tramway supervisor's, residence? This date was an evil day also for the steam enthusiast, with the end of regular steam out of Amiens Street.

With unusually impressive motive power for the 17.50 down/18.24 return, the latter leaves the up branch platform at Howth Junction on 27 April 1961, with No 174 and the UTA set, mentioned earlier on page 13. Who can now remember the palm trees on the centre platform? The landscape and railway five miles from Amiens Street, are now unrecognisable with the outward spread of the Dublin suburbs, and electrification of both main line and branch.

One of the pilgrim trains to Drogheda on that May Sunday in 1962 started from Antrim behind 'UG' No 45, formerly 78, the first of the class. The train will run to Lisburn and there reverse, a main-line engine (*Erne*) taking over. At Antrim, on the NCC main line, Great Northern trains used the bay platform seen here. Just short of the station is the junction used by the through workings, fairly frequent in summer, between the two railways. Indeed, a through Dublin–Portrush coach (or coaches; in 1939 a buffet car went as far as Antrim on Saturdays) was a feature for many years before 1940, slipped or detached from the 09.00 down express at Lisburn.

No 45 is passing the first station, or rather halt, after leaving Antrim. Millar's Bridge had hardly changed, apart from somewhat longer grass, since closure 18 months previously. There were no facilities other than a gravelled patch by the rails, and presumably the patrons used portable steps to access their trains. Nevertheless this was a timetabled halt, not merely a railcar request stop, with quite a reasonable service. The next station was Aldergrove, to which the NCC/UTA ran a daily train from Antrim for airport staff. The working timetable for the 1958/9 winter (the first to be issued after the division of the GNR, published entirely in that company's format apart from the title on the cover), has a remarkable entry relating to the evening working: the up 17.15 diesel railcar service to be "Banked from Antrim to Aldergrove by engine and coaches", ie the empty stock for the Aldergrove staff train. Do any photos exist of this most unusual operation? I wonder if any passengers in the back of the railcar had a close-up view of the smokebox of a working locomotive, or did the engine bring up the rear of the whole procession? The latter seems more likely, as only four minutes were allowed from arrival of the cavalcade to departure of the steam portion in the other direction.

Legatiriff, opened during the wartime period of heavy traffic, was a slightly more sophisticated establishment than Millar's Bridge, but still an unmanned halt. The accommodation would no doubt be a candidate for restoration today.

No 45 and her train join the main line at Knockmore Junction, the signal cabin being out of shot to the right, on the far side of the line. The Newforge siding, all that remains of the Banbridge line, diverges to the left, and was lifted later in 1962. The sign for the 25 mph limit over the Antrim branch can be seen by the junction, and accounts for the photographers' ability to outpace the train.

The Warrenpoint branch was above all a resort for summer Sundays, when it was busy with both the timetabled service and special excursion traffic. Otherwise the line was quiet beyond Newry, indeed quiet to a fault in winter, with no Sunday trains in our period and only a skeletal weekday service before final closure in 1965. Freight traffic remained to the end, and 'U' 66 ex-201 *Meath* is climbing the bank approaching Goraghwood with the afternoon goods on 19 March 1962.

By 1963 *Meath* has received a York Road overhaul and repaint, though now the lack of cleaning is becoming all too evident. She has also exchanged her 1948 roller-bearing tender for a much older B4 type, perhaps one of those built for one of the original 'U's of 1915. She is standing at Newry's not unimpressive, if now shabby, Edward Street station with an afternoon train from Goraghwood in August 1963. Newry had by now lost two railways, if we include the Bessbrook and Newry Tramway, which terminated close to Edward Street. The other was the Dundalk, Newry & Greenore (worked from 1933 by the GNR despite its continuing cross-Channel ownership), and the former complex of lines was in course of simplification.

On 27 August 1961 Adelaide's Driver Brammeld, with the Sunday 18.45 from Warrenpoint to Belfast and No 68, ex-205 *Down*, waits for the Newry North starter to clear. *Down* is still in blue, but when the summer traffic is over will be visiting York Road for overhaul and repaint. Scrapped in 1965, she deserved a better fate, as the very last ever to

be built of that long line of inside cylinder 4-4-0 passenger locomotives which had served many of the world's railways for almost a century.

The line through Newry was beset by level crossings, though evidently not much traffic on Bridge Street is held up by the passage of one of the 1948 'UG's, 48 ex-146, on her way to the Albert Basin by way of the Canal Branch on 9 December 1961.

Coal was still being imported by sea and transhipped, and unloading from a vessel in Albert Basin is in progress as No 48 moves her wagons slowly back under the cranes. This activity continued until the end of the branch in January 1965.

Newry's King Street signal box controlled not only the level crossing but the junction between the Warrenpoint line itself (diverging to the left) and the Canal branch, leading also to the DN&GR's end-on junction with the Great Northern, to the right. The former ran over GNR metals to Edward Street. This shot shows the dismal scene in August 1964. By then the writing was finally on the wall and the 'Jeeps', once barred from the branch, were now allowed to Warrenpoint, with evident indifference about their effect on the track, or vice versa. A dingy No 54 is working a return excursion from 'the Point'.

The scenery on the branch – mountain, woods and water – was of course one of the main attractions. From Newry onwards the line ran beside the tidal upper waters of the Newry River, discharging into Carlingford Lough at Warrenpoint. For the first five miles from Newry the river runs through Northern territory, but the frontier then comes down to the water on the west bank. It has to be admitted that one of the attractions of Warrenpoint on a Sunday was the possibility of a ferry trip from the 'dry' North across the estuary to the pubs of Omeath. Here No 48 makes her way through the woods just before Narrow Water.

No 48 is seen later in the evening hurrying the trippers homeward. Warrenpoint distant signal is in the background, and Narrow Water Castle dominates the view. A rowing boat ferry operated from beside the castle, and it was necessary to station a Customs officer there to control imports, perhaps mainly of alcohol, from the Republic.

The need for the presence of HM Customs must have been reduced after the closure of Narrow Water halt in 1959, but an officer was still in post two years later. This is the view from the foot of the castle looking north, with No 63 passing with a heavy excursion on 13 August 1961.

Payment of 1/- (5p) allowed access to the top of the castle, giving a fine view of the line. This is No 63 again, two weeks after the previous shot, while the ferryman is just getting under way from the slip. The dense line of cars on the road in the background suggests the looming fate of the railway.

This is the classic scene at 'the Point' on a summer Sunday evening, spoilt only by the inappropriate presence of the ex-NCC intruders. The only GN passenger engines unable to visit Warrenpoint were the compounds and 'VS's'; 'S' and 'S2's needed a short tender if they were to use the turntable.

The Derry Road

The 'Derry Road', the line from Portadown to Londonderry by way of Dungannon, Omagh and Strabane, held a firm place in the affections of many enthusiasts and was highly valued by the inhabitants of the region it served, who so strongly resisted its eventual closure on 14 February 1965. It was a route of particular difficulty, characterised by awkward gradients and curvature, but could compete for traffic between Ulster's two principal cities until the NCC opened their direct Greenisland cut-off in 1934. That was no help to those travelling from intermediate stations on the GN line, nor indeed to the people of Donegal who lost their access to Dublin and the south via Strabane. But a decent service continued to the end in the face of declining standards of maintenance, both of track and rolling stock. By our time a 45 mph speed limit had been imposed for steam traction – not widely observed, it must be said, by drivers interested in timekeeping, further hampered by the singling of certain sections. Traffic in summer, which saw most steam working, tested the line's capacity to the limit in its later years, after the loss of some passing loops.

At Dungannon on 26 June 1961, 'S' No 61, ex-173, *Galteemore*, runs in with the summer steam-worked 10.30 from Derry. The fireman is about to take the single-line staff for the section to Trew & Moy. The train is on time, is crossing the 11.15 diesel from Belfast standing at the other platform as booked, and the Derry driver is about to hand over to Bob Surgeon, one of Belfast's hardest runners. The size and weight of the GN staffs made slow speed very necessary at passing points. In earlier days, the tenders of engines working on the Derry line were fitted with catchers, in the form of nets somewhat reminiscent of those used on Post Office sorting vans. 173/61 was the first 'S' to be renewed, in 1938, and her reputation was perhaps the highest of the class, but she was not given an overhaul by the UTA, an omission that they may later have regretted. A couple of weeks after this photo was taken I travelled in both directions over the Derry line on two successive days, on which 61 ('S') and 62 ('S2') were handled by the same four crews on the same duties with the same loads: 61, nearing the end of her days, was slightly the faster at all points, although 62 was fresh from York Road shops. Perhaps this result supports the belief in the slight inferiority of the 'S2' sub-class, unless it is a comment on the practices at the NCC's works. The old CIÉ van on the rear of the 11.15 (No 292 again?) is probably sealed, containing 'Free to Free' traffic from stations south of the Border, for Donegal.

The Derry Road ran through almost continuously attractive countryside. On a fine Sunday morning between Dungannon and Pomeroy, Jack Fowler, a senior driver at Portadown, is spending a profitable and not unduly strenuous day in charge of a big 'SG3' 0-6-0 (No 35, ex-GN 41), generous motive power for a few wagons on a day spent replacing sleepers – so some track maintenance was still being undertaken in July 1962. The curve in the background carries one of the many permanent speed restrictions, this one to 30 mph.

Above Pomeroy the climbing steepens to the summit at milepost 26½, the highest point (at 561 feet) on the Great Northern lines since the closure in 1923 of the Armagh–Castleblayney section with its summit near Carnagh 52 feet higher. In August 1963, a grimy No 60, *Slieve Donard* (formerly 172)

emerges on to the moors at the top of the bank from Carrickmore with a morning train from Derry. The boggy nature of the terrain is apparent, and its effect on the track, as well as the constant curvature, accounts for the dictum of George Glover, the GNR's long-serving Chief Mechanical Engineer, that no engine should work on the line for more than six months!

NCC engines had been permitted on the Derry road, subject to a 30 mph restriction, by 1963 – initially 'Moguls' on goods trains, and in the line's final year, 1964, 'Jeeps' on anything. Here is one of the latter running down the 1 in 72 from the summit towards Carrickmore on a train for Omagh and Derry – timekeeping is unlikely even with some disregard of that overall speed limit, for which no allowance was made in the timetable.

On 26 June 1961 *Slievenamon* is ready to leave Omagh for Derry with the 14.45 from Belfast. She has had a recent overhaul and looks good, but had been an uninspiring performer on this day. In the past, Omagh was an important railway centre and had been a District headquarters, but had lost its Superintendent in 1953, even before the closure of the 'Irish North' lines four years later. On the locomotive side, though the shed was closed by our time, there was still a small establishment of enginemen, amongst whom the name of driver Barney McGirr comes particularly to mind. The station served a considerable rural hinterland, and goods traffic was still tolerably heavy.

The annual 'Apprentice Boys' celebrations in Derry, a relatively peaceful occasion in those years, always produced several specials. On 10 August 1964 an unidentified 'SG2' is trundling the empty stock for such a train across one of the many crossings of the River Mourne between the minor summit near Mountjoy halt and Strabane. The train will pick up its load of not necessarily youthful celebrants at Omagh for the day's outing to Derry.

Two years earlier, the UTA was curiously short of motive power, hence the purchase of the redundant engines from CIÉ in 1963. The Derry line had been reliant on the smaller 'U' and 'UG' locomotives which were often in difficulties on the harder parts of the road. North of Omagh the gradients and timings were easier, and this is No 47 at Sion Mills with an empty train for the Apprentice Boys on 10 August 1962. This was a place of some consequence thanks to Herdman's linen mills, on the right, which generated both goods and passenger traffic, the latter including a short working to Strabane for the mill workers. A wagon turntable gave access to the mill itself. Sion Mills was effectively a 'company' village, and, untypically for Tyrone, fielded a cricket team. The ground was the scene of an even less typical Irish victory over a West Indian side in 1969.

Strabane had lost its railway to Donegal (the County Donegal 3ft-gauge system) in January 1959, though passengers did use connecting buses for the remaining life of the Derry Road. There are still grass-grown tracks by the Donegal platforms to the left, on 7 August 1961. Both the station and *Galteemore,* on the 10.30 Derry–Belfast, look well-worn, but Driver Pentland of Derry was to demonstrate that appearances could be deceptive.

Nevertheless, County Donegal still had three active stations on the GN line to Derry, even if the trains were operated by another country's nationalised railway: CIÉ were the owners of Porthall, St Johnston and Carrigans, on the west bank of the Foyle. St Johnston was the significant one of the three, with passing loop and siding accommodation for 'Free to Free' traffic in sealed vans. The white-capped Irish Customs officer supervises the call of an Omagh–Derry train on 10 August 1962. No 48's fireman seems to be still clutching the St Johnston–Derry staff which he has snatched from the signalman, necessary since the singling of the line on to Derry in 1933.

The Bangor Line

No doubt the Bangor line should not be considered an outpost of the Great Northern, even if that company had been involved in the affairs of the Belfast and County Down Railway (BCDR) for some years. But no County Down engines were left after 1953; the only steam trains to be found in the 1960s on the surviving stump, the characterful twelve-mile line from Queen's Quay to Bangor, were hauled by the smaller locomotives of the GNR, the 'U's and their 0-6-0 counterparts, the 'UG's. There was in fact quite a heavy excursion traffic in summer from other sections of the UTA lines: Sunday School outings in spring, and occasional through specials from further afield, including a high-summer weekly excursion from Bangor to Dublin. All these workings joined the Bangor line at Ballymacarrett Junction, half a mile from Queen's Quay terminus, normally changing from a main-line engine at Maysfields yard for something light enough to cross the 'shaky' Lagan bridge. I travelled on the line only twice by steam: most notably in 1960 on a Royal Black Preceptory special from Portadown, where I'd spent the night of the 12th July! I travelled in the brake van, and 'UG' 48 performed quite creditably, running non-stop from Lisburn, and with a substantial eight-coach train tackling the rather brutal 2½-mile Holywood bank in decent style. Photographic trips to the line were a welcome activity in spring, before the full summer timetable increased the opportunities elsewhere.

Bangor terminus, and No 49 starts a return Sunday School outing away up the bank to Bangor West on a June evening in 1962. The 'UG's were the preferred engines for the line – with no turntable at Bangor, 4-4-0s running tender-first, with less adhesion and no back sand, could slip and stall on the 1 in 72 climb from Holywood, and were latterly banned unless assistance was available.

Two weeks after the previous shot, 'UG's meet at Craigavad – No 49 (left) of the 1948 build, and on a down train, No 45 of 1937 running with an older replacement tender. Both have by now received an overhaul and repaint at York Road.

On the other hand No 67, ex-202 *Louth*, though renumbered, is still in blue; she is running (before the edict mentioned above) with an up train over the Crawfordsburn viaduct, the principal engineering work of the line.

The BCDR in its prosperous days built imposing stations, in this case Helen's Bay, with 49 again on a Sunday School outing for Bangor.

No 49, fresh from the shops, seemed a favourite choice in 1962, and the fireman appears relaxed while the engine deals competently with the 1 in 72 climb from Holywood, approaching Marino station. Note the banner signal characteristic of the line.

And here the same engine runs back down the bank, with steam shut off and some to spare. Marino station is fortunate to have survived, having closed in 1957 but reopening after justifiable second thoughts in 1960.

A Southern Steam Survival:
Ballast Workings on CIÉ Lines

Weather permitting, there was one reliable resource for camera-toting steam enthusiasts with their own transport. All the year round, ballast was supplied from CIÉ's two quarries to all parts of the system: Lisduff, close to that station on the Cork main line six miles south of Ballybrophy, and Lecarrow, eight miles beyond Athlone on the Mayo branch. The products ('stone', 'screenings' and 'chippings') of the former served mainly ex-GS&W and ex-D&SER lines, and of the latter, those of the former MGW (the 'Midland'). Accordingly two trains were based at Lisduff and one at Lecarrow. These trains had regular crews with specialised guards in charge, and conveyed brake vans, usually one at each end, equipped for spreading ('teeming') the ballast and also with creature comforts for the crews, who might be away for two or even three days depending on destination. Diesel locomotives could not be spared for these unhurried operations, for the trains received low priority on the line, and steam power was provided by Thurles shed (Lisduff) and Athlone (Lecarrow), with drivers of necessarily wide route knowledge. The three ballast guards were well-known on the system: Tom Harney on the Lecarrow train, Joe Lacumber on the Lisduff No 1, and the third, anonymous as far as we were concerned, on Lisduff No 2. The weekly circular (marked 'Confidential' – but not excessively so) gave destinations for the week, but without timings, arranged *ad hoc* to be clear of timetabled traffic. Given a map then, it was not difficult to outpace a ballast. We will follow two or three of these expeditions.

The crusher at Lisduff quarry was supplied by aerial ropeway, and the rail access was by a facing junction from the down main line, leading also to sidings for storing the ballast hoppers. The engine supplied by Thurles was often, as here, an unrebuilt (or perhaps better, 'unsuperheated') 'J15'. This famous class hardly needs an introduction. One of the last to be withdrawn in 1965, No 151, entered service in 1868, and the 'J15's remained by far the most numerous class in the country for 87 years. The unrebuilt engines looked much more slender than those, the majority, which had received superheaters from 1930. The boilers were in fact of the same diameter, but the bulkier smokebox and Belpaire firebox made the rebuilds seem bigger, and indeed increased weight by almost three tons, to 33½ tons. The 'J15's were built from 1867 to 1903, and our first sight of the class is of No 232, of the last batch, seen under the crusher in March 1961.

On Sunday 29 October 1961 another 'unrebuilt', No 195, is about to take the Lisduff No 2 train out for a three-day operation to discharge ballast on the south-eastern section near Enniscorthy – a long round, with an overnight stop in Dublin, and we shall pursue her for the first two days. She has just arrived from Thurles, fourteen miles south of Lisduff, with the empty hoppers which she is now reversing off the up main line into the sidings. There is an additional wagon next to the engine, to be shunted off before the train can be loaded for departure.

The empty train is now being cautiously reversed under the crusher for loading, after which it will be drawn forward on to the up main line and away to Dublin and the south-east.

No 195 is now making her way up the Cork main line, past Monasterevan. The low platforms and faintly ecclesiastical characteristics typify the architect Sancton Wood's designs for stations on the GS&WR's main line.

Hazelhatch station was closed at this time, but now has a successor very much open, on the newly-quadrupled Dublin suburban section of the main line, unrecognisable from the scene shown here. There are three people on the engine, and I doubt if it is the official driver who is visible on the left, driver's, side. The discomforts of the 'J15' cab are somewhat alleviated in the usual way, by the wooden batten jammed under the handrail as an improvised armrest – the cab side sheet has an uncompromising cut-out without so much as a beading to soften the edge.

It is now the following morning, Monday, and the loaded train is climbing to Bray Head, with the town in the background. The grassy platform beside the engine is all that remains of Naylor's Cove halt, open briefly around 1906 for patrons of the seawater swimming baths nearby.

No 195 is at grips with the climb to the summit of the south-eastern main line. The train has just topped the three miles at 1 in 100 / 1 in 90 and has a brief respite through Glenealy station before the final stretch to the top. The fireman can then take it easy for twelve miles or so, down the Vale of Avoca, before the more sawtooth profile of the line onwards to Enniscorthy.

Autumn tints – No 195 and train on one of the several crossings of the Avonmore River on the descent from Rathdrum to Avoca.

Woodenbridge station, junction for the Shillelagh branch which succumbed in 1944 in the difficult conditions of that period (the 'Emergency'), when coal supplies were almost non-existent and train services became dependent on turf, timber, and/or the 'duff', which was an unwholesome mixture involving cement and pitch. The branch diverged from the up side, using the platform face behind the buildings on the left. Woodenbridge station itself closed in 1964. No 195 still has thirty-odd miles to go to Enniscorthy with her loaded train, before engine and crew can turn for home, another day's journey away.

The Lecarrow train was normally headed by an ex-MGW engine based at Athlone. On a late autumn day in 1961, one of the Midland 'Cattle Engines', 'J5' No 639, led David Houston and me on a long drive westwards in pursuit of 'Tom Harney's Ballast'. There were 23 'J5's, imposing locomotives slightly smaller than the GNR's SG3s, introduced at much the same time (1922). They had driving wheels as large as 5'8", supposedly giving them a fair turn of speed and useful for mixed traffic working. The nickname arose from their use on reasonably fast livestock specials. No evidence of their speed potential came my way: I travelled behind only one, No 637, on an all-stations local from Amiens Street to Dun Laoghaire and back – hardly perhaps a fair test, with speed only once reaching 30 mph. In this scene Tom Harney is discussing the day's arrangements with the driver at Dublin's Liffey Junction, where the train has stabled overnight. The ballast is for North Wall yard, after which it will take the rest of the day to get the empties home again.

After running tender-first down to North Wall and discharging, the train (and the photographers' van) are poised for departure, back up the bank to Glasnevin Junction, Liffey Junction and then away homeward on the Midland main line.

Moyvalley station has had a recent and colourful repaint, the usual prelude to closure which came two years later. The line closely followed the course of the Royal Canal, including its curvature, and No 639 leans to the curve as the staffs are exchanged. The Midland line, mostly singled in 1929 for economy, used miniature staffs, much more manageable for catching by hand with their hoops than the massive affairs of the GNR, and I have witnessed hand exchange at 50 mph.

The ballasts spent a good deal of time waiting in loops for higher-priority traffic to pass. This is Hill of Down, by now like Moyvalley only a request stop for a single passenger service each way. The through road is set for a non-stop up train from Westport. No 639 is one of the majority of the class built by the MGWR at Broadstone, and it is notable that this relatively small company was capable of

producing eighteen quite large locomotives in its own workshops. The first five of the class had come from Armstrong-Whitworth, and that firm also supplied sets of frames and cylinders for five of the Broadstone examples. Later members of the class differed somewhat in appearance, with raised footplating clear of the crankpins.

Killucan was a typical Midland station, closed to passengers by this time, though its substantial goods shed was still in use. As the staff exchange shows, it was still an active block post.

The last shot of this series, taken as the shadows lengthen, shows the train looped again, four miles beyond Killucan at 46th-Mile Box. This block post divided the long section between Killucan and Mullingar, but although the track on the loop looks well-used, no trains at this period were booked to cross here. No doubt the facility was useful when delays caused problems on the single line.

Just after Mullingar the Royal Canal turned northwards to find a more level alignment towards the Shannon, while the now-closed Mullingar–Athlone section of the main line climbed to the modest summit near Castletown. The Lecarrow ballast is returning empty from Dublin past Bellmount level crossing, where railway and waterway finally part company. The engine, 'J18' No 613, is one of the MGW's equivalents to the GS&W's 'J15' 0-6-0s, which they resembled fairly closely after their rebuilding from the 1930s with Inchicore superheated boilers and, often, cabs.

No 613 is running past Streamstown, junction for the moribund Horseleap branch linking the MGW line with the G&SW at Clara. By May 1962 when these photos were taken, the line had for years been used only for wagon storage. The IRRS special of 18 March the next year was probably the last movement apart from the lifting train. The branch diverged in the down direction from the platform face behind the signalman waiting to receive the staff.

This is taken from the driver's side on the right, on these Midland engines. Two of the party had been beckoned aboard 613 at Moate, to be greeted with the enquiry "Do you drive?" – to which only one answer was possible. Midland men were accustomed to eccentrics who were prepared to take an interest in, if not actually share, their work, as the late Bob Clements had done for many years. The train is approaching 73rd-Mile Box, another intermediate block post and loop, usually switched out, and closed later in 1962.

After arrival at Athlone, 613 and train were shunted into one of the sidings at Athlone East, on the GS&W line from Portarlington. The passenger station here had been closed since 1925, to be reopened forty years later, after considerable refurbishment, with the transfer of Galway and Westport traffic to the route from Dublin Heuston (formerly Kingsbridge). Tom Harney has come forward to discuss the next move with the enginemen.

In early October 1962, one of the Lisduff trains was dispatched on a circular trip to work near Wexford, via Waterford and the North Wexford line of the former Dublin & South Eastern Railway. To cope with the steep gradients, two rebuilt 'J15's were provided, and Nos 183 and 116 are seen entering New Ross in the early morning with the loaded train.

After New Ross the second engine earns its keep, facing the three miles at 1 in 60 of Ballyanne bank, and here the two engines are at grips with the worst of the gradient but evidently have matters well in hand. At this precise spot, a famous incident of the Civil War took place in 1923. Republican forces were disrupting the railways in an attempt to isolate Waterford, and engine No 17 of the D&SER was derailed on the embankment close to the bridge. The intention was to send it down to the road below, but No 17 remained at the top, precariously balanced with no prospect of re-railing in situ. Eventually the engine was skidded down the embankment on its side on a sleeper ramp, and then righted and actually steamed on portable track along the road for a mile before regaining the level beside the line. By extraordinary coincidence No 17 had found herself on a road before: this was the engine which in 1900 burst through the end wall of Harcourt Street Station in Dublin, dangling above Hatch Street until lowered on to the roadway below. On that occasion however she does not seem to have returned home under her own steam.

After Palace East, that curiously named and situated station approached by a steep bank in both directions, eastbound trains can take it easy. In steam days most would need to use the big water tower at the far end of the curious triangular platform, the near face where the ballast is standing being used by D&SE trains for Wexford and – a long time ago – the far side by those coming off the GS&W line from Bagenalstown (Muine Bheag), which terminated here.

City and Suburban:
A look around the purlieus of Belfast and Dublin

Steam activity in the 1960s was, unsurprisingly, most prolific – and accessible to the enthusiast – in and around the major cities. Steam worked regularly on suburban passenger services out of Belfast towards Larne and Portadown, to supplement first-generation diesels. Dublin's Great Northern and South-Eastern commuter routes were less reliant on steam, but saw quite frequent substitutions to cover non-availability of more modern power. In both cities it was possible to find steam locomotives at work on shunting and local freight work, not least in the docklands. Alas, the days when Cork boasted no less than five railways with their own passenger termini were long gone, and although steam on mundane duties continued there till the end came in 1963, the 330 mile round trip from Dublin meant fewer opportunities for the photographer.

We start in Belfast, where the former NCC's workshops almost adjoined York Road terminus. After 1958, any UTA ex-GNR(I) engines needing works attention had to go to York Road (via Antrim), and, as we have already seen, received the rather smart UTA lined livery after a general overhaul. It was usual for ex-works engines to be run in on station pilot duties, and here it is 'SG' No 43, ex-175, a few days out of the shops and a bit dusty but with immaculate paintwork. Occasionally they were used on a train; it is recorded that No 33 ex-20, an 'SG3', ran the evening boat express to Larne Harbour on 26 July 1963.

This shot could be described as a scoop: the first and only visit of a 'VS' to the NCC lines. The giveaway is the typical Berkeley Deane Wise architecture of Whiteabbey station. On 22 March 1962 I had come down on the Thursday 08.45 excursion from Dublin.

This was a lively run behind No 207, driven by Ned O'Grady, whose father Dick had fired to the great Micky O' Farrell on some of the most exciting runs of the 1932 accelerations. On the concourse of Great Victoria Street I met an Adelaide fireman who told me I'd just missed seeing 58 departing for Antrim and York Road, for remedial work on her firebox. Luckily I had the camera, and plenty of time to reach Whiteabbey!

In September 1962 the last NCC 4-4-0, U2 No 74 *Dunluce Castle*, waits outside York Road shops, for cosmetic restoration and preservation. Possibly her last use was in June 1961, on the joint enthusiasts' railtour of Ireland, but she can now be seen in all her crimson glory at the Cultra museum. Beside her is the tender of one of the GNR 'U's in the shops for overhaul and repaint.

In March 1962 the last regauged 'Jinty', 0-6-0T No 19, was dead at York Road and I don't think worked again before withdrawal the following year. She and her one sister came from the parent LMS in 1944 to alleviate the then desperate locomotive shortage. They were occasionally used on local passenger services, but were later reduced to shunting. Note the UTA lorry with snowplough and chains on the rear wheels; hardly for use on conventional rails, but perhaps adequate for clearing the tram track on the dock lines?

That March day in 1962 proved productive. After returning from Whiteabbey I spent some time walking round the dock lines on the west side of the harbour, first encountering the last active NCC 0-6-0, No 13. Her tender looks antique, but she was built in 1923 and rebuilt with a Belpaire boiler as 'recently' as 1953.

Another notable shunter was numberless under her original SL&NCR ownership, 0-6-4T *Lough Erne*, now UTA No 27, and presumably the last 'long boiler' locomotive ever built (in 1949, despite her appearance). Her builders, Beyer Peacock, supplied her and her sister *Lough Melvin* reluctantly to her first owners under a hire purchase arrangement, the company being quite unable to meet the capital cost. The UTA bought them from Beyers in 1959. She is seen diving into the subway beneath the Queen's Bridge with a transfer from the docks to the GN's Maysfields yards.

And here ex-GN 'PG' 0-6-0 No 10, built in 1904 and last survivor of her class, emerges from the other end of the subway. Concerns about overhead clearances, which led to the building of the 'RT' class 0-6-4 tanks with reduced boiler mountings for working the dock lines, seem to have evaporated by our period.

No 10 (once named *Bessbrook*) goes head to head with one of the vehicles which supplanted her and her ilk. She is negotiating what must surely have been Ireland's only double-track triangular junction, though not subject to any formal signalling or other arrangements, where the connection between the Harbour Commisssioners' lines and the NCC was made by way of Dufferin Dock Junction and Duncrue Street.

A reminder that even in the 1960s steam in another form was present around the docks. The haulage firm Harkness still had a couple of traction engines, and some horses, at work. I once visited the shed, or stables, which they shared – the residents were all out at work, but their stalls each held a small heap of either ashes or horse droppings, as appropriate!

There was still a healthy, partly steam-worked, suburban service on the GN line from Belfast to Lisburn and Portadown. The 'T1'/'T2' class 4-4-2 tanks were well suited to the job, but few were left by the 1960s. No 187 is acting as Great Victoria Street station pilot on 7 October 1961.

Almost any type of engine turned up on Lisburn locals, and with up to seven stops in less than eight miles, good acceleration was more use than maximum speed. Not all the locals did stop everywhere, and certainly 'UG' 49 is not going to do so at Balmoral on an April morning in 1962.

Nothing very remarkable about an 'SG2' (UTA 38, formerly GN 16) on a lunchtime Lisburn local, at Derriaghy on 6 August 1962. What is a bit odd is that the guard, waiting to wave the train away, is a CIÉ man – George Brien, from the South-Eastern section at that – who has already worked the 08.45 excursion down from Dublin and will do duty again on the 17.50 return. I didn't enquire about any accountants' involvement in this arrangement, or whether, perhaps more likely, George was just standing in to oblige. Derriaghy Halt was lucky to have survived, reopening in 1956 by public demand after a three-year closure.

We now move south to Dublin. First, a conversation piece at Kingsbridge (now Heuston) Station, in May 1961. No steam passenger trains then worked into the station, except the staff shuttle from Inchicore works, here headed by an unlikely engine, ex-GN 'JT' 2-4-2T No 91, sole survivor of its class thanks to a fairly recent overhaul as the regular power on the GN's Belturbet branch, closed in 1957. No 91 had just taken over the Inchicore job from another 2-4-2T , GS&WR No 42, dating from 1893: the last passenger design of HA Ivatt to survive anywhere in company service. The staff did not travel in the latest products of Inchicore works!

Amiens Street (Connolly) Station, 26 July 1962: a very unusual sight, a 'UG' about to set off at 19.40 on a 125-mile trip, non-stop to Goraghwood (72 miles), thence on to Bangor, the return working of the excursion traditionally run to Dublin on summer Thursdays. No 47 (ex-82) was one of the 1937 'UG's, now matched with a new tender, but only of 2500-gallon capacity. The UTA were inexplicably short of locomotives, and Adelaide's Jimmy Shields had to manage with this unsuitable machine. Some of us travelled as far as Goraghwood, and were pleased to record a 60 mph burst before Dundalk and a very fair climb to Adavoyle, but the excursionists in their vintage coaches were probably glad to reach Bangor and get to bed.

Operation of the 'All-in' specials (travel, meals and match ticket) from Belfast for Rugby International games at Lansdowne Road was a prestige affair. The up train ran through, changing engines at Amiens Street (the 'VS' being too heavy to cross the Liffey) for the two miles on to Lansdowne Road station. In December 1960 *Lagan* takes the second of two crossovers, from the Great Northern main line to CIÉ's Loop Line platform at Amiens Street. The trilby hat visible behind the driver must surely be worn by Billy Hanley, the UTA's much-respected locomotive inspector. Senior members of the UTA hierarchy were usually among the passengers, with some consequences in the 1963 season. By that time *Lagan*, over four years out of shops, was not fit to work a heavy non-stop train, and it was deemed necessary to borrow (or hire, no doubt) *Boyne* from CIÉ. The ignominy was evidently keenly felt, and for the next match *Lagan* was fettled up somewhat, the load was reduced, and a CIÉ boiler van was loaned/ hired to provide the steam heat; and the job was given to Adelaide's Bob Surgeon, a dab hand with a 'VS'. I scrounged a seat at the back of the return train, and Surgeon duly ran it sharp to time. I was talking to the crew at Belfast when a well-dined passenger – evidently a UTA officer but no railwayman – came up to demand of Bob, "Is this one of *our* Board's engines?", and was evidently reassured by the answer!

When the amalgamation of all the railways in the Republic took place in 1925, to form the Great Southern Railways Company, the 'Woolwich' 2-6-0s then in course of assembly at the MGWR's Broadstone works were effectively the only modern locomotives in Ireland. Re-gauged versions of the Southern Railway's 'N' and 'U' class, they were a fully up-to-date mixed traffic locomotive, widely used on main-line passenger as well as goods services until the diesel invasion. By our time almost all had gone; here No 376, last to survive in the Dublin area, is in dismal order and reduced to shunting North Wall yards in January 1961 a few months before withdrawal. Note the staff catcher still in place on the cabside, for working over the Midland main line.

The MGW main line's intimate connection with the Royal Canal started at Liffey Junction, where the pilot engine, a Midland survivor ('J26' 0-6-0T No 562) is standing on the 'Liffey Branch' which at first gave access to the MGW North Wall yard, later via Newcomen Junction to Amiens Street and the DSER, and subsequently, from 1937, also by the easier route via the remodelled Glasnevin Junction. The original main line to Broadstone station, closed in 1937, kept to the south side of the canal, passing behind the signal box.

Liffey Junction had an occasional passenger service until the 1937 alterations, when trains were diverted to Amiens Street and Westland Row. The platforms and buildings were in existence when these photos were taken in February 1961.

Inchicore platform served the works staff, and briefly, when the GS&WR's 1877 Link Line was extended via Drumcondra in 1901, had a public passenger service to Amiens Street. Here on 11 February 1962 a loaded Lisduff ballast train is bound for the link line with an unidentified 'J9' 0-6-0 in charge; this class of eight engines, effectively enlarged 'J15s', was introduced in 1903, superheated in the 1930s with Belpaire boilers, and all but two lasted into the 1960s. Note, in the background, one of the 'Rosslare' set of twelve-wheel clerestory coaches dating from 1907. The only one I ever saw at work was the diner, No 353, in a Waterford–Dundalk football special in early 1959 (hauled from Dublin by GN compound No 85!).

The ballast has now turned left at Islandbridge Junction on to the link line, is crossing the Liffey, and is about to pass under Conyngham Road into Phoenix Park tunnel. Kingsbridge (Heuston) station is out of shot to the left; the tower in the background belongs to the Royal Hospital. Despite appearances I don't remember the train being banked, least of all by steam – no steam pilot was rostered at Kingsbridge, certainly not on a Sunday. Could that plume be exhaust from an ill-conditioned Metrovick diesel…?

This may look like a bit like a high-speed main line, but is actually the link line at Cabra yard, seen in November 1961 with an ex-GNR 0-6-0 shunting the sidings, laid out for the reception of livestock traffic when the line was opened in 1877 and latterly becoming a cement terminal.

Rail-over-rail bridges are scarce in Ireland: here the link line passes under the Liffey Branch of the former MGWR, on which the loaded Lecarrow ballast which we saw earlier is making its way down to unload at North Wall behind tender-first No 639. The round tower in Glasnevin Cemetery is in the background. Soon after the underbridge the link line will curve to the right and be joined by the connection from the MGW main line at Glasnevin Junction.

The key to the complex railway geography and history of North Dublin is Glasnevin Junction, where we see No 639 hauling its now-empty train back up to Liffey Junction. Originally the connection here allowed GS&W trains to run from the link line to North Wall, via the Midland's Liffey branch, and (from 1892) by the awkward line from Newcomen Junction to Amiens Street, Westland Row, and Kingstown/ Dun Laoghaire for passengers and the mails. In 1901 the junction became disused when the GS&W at last opened its own easier route via Drumcondra, and

in 1937 the connection was reinstated but reversed, enabling trains from the Midland to run to Amiens Street and Westland Row, and Broadstone Station to be closed. To the left of the engine is the connection from the MGW main line to the Drumcondra Link. To the left of that again, the link line itself comes in, having passed *under* the MGW, as seen above. On the far right of this shot is the short branch, or long siding, from Liffey Junction to the North City Mills.

Drumcondra lost its passenger service in 1910, and no trace of platforms remained when the 'J9' and its ballast passed the site in 1962. But the brick buildings survived at street level, for some time serving as the headquarters of the Irish Railway Record Society, and are now again incorporated in the station, reopened in 1998 and now part of the Western Commuter system. In 2017 a new service was inaugurated from the new Grand Canal Dock station, through the refurbished Phoenix Park tunnel to suburban stations on the Cork main line.

In the 1960s, Dublin suburban developments, and consequent train services, hardly extended beyond the coastal areas served by the GNR and former D&SER lines. We have already glimpsed the former; the South-Eastern section saw little steam other than the Dun Laoghaire Pier–Westland Row boat trains, which remained steam to the end, handled by almost any engine fit to run the six-and-a-half miles, from 'J15's to the occasional ex-GN 'S'. There was however an Amiens Street to Greystones Saturday steam-worked lunchtime train throughout much of our period, fast to Dun Laoghaire, attractive to enthusiasts both for travelling and photography, and ex-GN 'Q' 132 was a favourite performer. On 10 February 1962 it was thought desirable to combine both interests, so by pre-positioning the van by the exit at Dun Laoghaire it was possible to disembark, drive smartly the three-quarters of a mile to Sandycove, photograph the train entering, and resume our original seats; an exercise hardly commendable then, through 1962 traffic, and certainly best not attempted now.

This is Woodbrook halt, a mile north of Bray, used only occasionally for traffic to the adjacent championship golf course. No 132 is passing with that 13.10 Amiens Street–Greystones, photographed by a teenage David Houston on the platform. The inland line to Harcourt Street was closed nearly three years earlier, but a skeletal distant signal post still guards the approach to the one-time Shanganagh Junction.

On the 23 September 1961, David might have been helping the fireman to turn 132 at Greystones…

…and here Driver Everard is waiting for the last passengers to board and to depart on the return trip.

Various engines worked the Greystones trip before No 132 took over. Here it is another GN machine, 'SG2' No 184, rounding Bray Head northbound. This spectacular section, originally engineered by Brunel himself, was subject to erosion and required realignment more than once; that in 1917 included the boring of a new tunnel, the third longest in the country. One of the earlier disused tunnels is visible in the distance.

Tender engines needed a refill on the Greystones round, and on this blustery 11 February 1961 it is again No 184, with Driver Hannay topping up at Bray on the return leg. Bray station shared with Dun Laoghaire the inconvenience of a single platform for all trains, until rebuilt in 1927. Dun Laoghaire was, extraordinarily, not remodelled until 1957, though local trains terminating there had the use of the original bay platform of the Dublin & Kingstown station.

An early morning scene in April 1962 at Carlisle Pier, Dun Laoghaire. The mailboat *Cambria* has arrived from Holyhead, the boat train has loaded and is departing behind 'U' No 199. Another ex-GN engine is waiting, perhaps to work the later 'Parcel Post'.

And here in October 1961 is the 'Parcel Post', leaving the pier and passing the Royal St George, one of Dun Laoghaire's three distinguished yacht clubs. The engine is the very last surviving passenger locomotive of the GS&WR, 'D11' No 301 of 1900, once *Victoria,* a rare named G&SWR locomotive – a contemporary of the GN's 'Q' class. Thought to have been withdrawn, 301 was resurrected in the spring of 1961 to work through flooding at Ballycar, near Limerick, and after the waters subsided returned to Dublin and found useful employment for another few months on gentle local duties. In October of that year she operated a memorable enthusiasts' excursion, an ambitious round trip from Dublin to Waterford via Rosslare and back by Kilkenny and

Carlow – not altogether trouble-free, with eventual return to Dublin at 00.01 (though not exceptional in this respect: who remembers returning from West Cork on St Patrick's Day 1961, when the diner started supper service after leaving Cork for Dublin at 00.04?). But old 301, after various misadventures, finished with a fine spin homeward from Kildare – I recall Driver Neville's unprintable comment on being pulled up from 65 mph to stop at Hazelhatch to set down Bob Clements, "a good friend – but tonight…"

A gap in the wall at the back of Dun Laoghaire station gave access to the harbourside yard of the Commissioners of Irish Lights, responsible for the buoyage and lighting of Irish waters. No 199 has been commandeered from a local passenger working to do some shunting in the yard. The station signalbox is in the background, built on the platform separating the down through line from the former Dublin & Kingstown terminus on the left.

The South-Eastern line at Lansdowne Road actually passes under the west stand of the Rugby ground, though the station has no cover for alighting spectators. 'S' No 170 *Errigal* is unusual power for a down local in February 1962, but she did some work on this section, including at least one boat train trip.

This is *Errigal* again, only a short distance from Lansdowne Road – she is at the head of a train of horseboxes in the Royal Dublin Society's sidings at Ballsbridge, with the RDS building in the background. The Society was, and is, at the forefront of agricultural and intellectual life in Ireland, having been addressed in the past by both Cecil J Allen and OS Nock on railway subjects! The horseboxes rather than the adjacent cattle trucks certainly suggest an equine event, but the date in February 1962 relates to the RDS Bull and Pig Show, for which a number of specials were run. Maybe this train was to form Special No 76 to Limerick Junction, which according to the weekly circular "must be dispatched on time and hurried on…", to keep clear of following passenger traffic. Our sympathies are perhaps with the bulls (or pigs).

Errigal was probably unique in having worked in company service on all the major systems of the Irish network. We have just seen her on the South-Eastern section of CIÉ; she had represented the GNR(I) for a week on the NCC in the exchanges of 1935. I rode on her to Athlone on the Midland in December 1961 on the 'turkey train', the regular Christmas perishable working. Here she is on 7 November 1961 passing Kildare, on the 'trial train' operated on Fridays at passenger train speeds from Inchicore works, down the Cork line to Portlaoise or Thurles with recently-repaired coaching stock.

Engines of GS&W, or indeed GSR, origin on passenger trains were unusual sights by 1960, and it was a treat to find a 'J4' working the Greystones turn on 18 February 1961. The J4s were the highly-regarded ultimate development of the G&SW 0-6-0, and there were eight of them, built new with superheaters in 1913/14 and all lasting till the 1960s. The design was attributed to Richard Maunsell, but in most respects followed previous Inchicore practice. A close look at 261's tender reveals the remains of green livery, perhaps inherited from a 400-class 4-6-0. The fireman is brewing up at Dun Laoghaire on the return from Greystones.

I seem to recall that the vigorous start from Dun Laoghaire was a conscious effort by Driver Molloy to outpace the photographers…

…however, note that grubby black van, already parked under the Gardiner Street Lower bridge behind the Custom House, as No 261 crosses on the Loop Line approach to Amiens Street.

The Unchanged Scene:
Some of CIÉ's Rural Survivals

The only way to be sure of travelling behind a locomotive of the former GSR or its predecessors was to visit one of the more remote CIÉ branches to remain regularly steam-worked. By the 1960s these were indeed few and far between, and the Working Timetable no longer included the telltale 'Steam' or 'Loco J' (referring to power class, not the Whyte wheel notation) heading, even for those lines. There were a few other services where there was tacit acceptance that steam substitution was necessary, and the WTT was discreetly silent. By now such trains would normally consist of a bogie coach, sometimes still supplemented by one or more six-wheelers; occasionally the latter were the only option.

Ballaghaderreen was connected to the outside world by the 'Morning Branch', on which the last train ran at 13.00 from Kilfree Junction, on the MGW's Sligo line, with the Dublin mails and (if any) passengers. Modernisation had passed the line by, as indicated by the signalling at Edmondstown, one of the two intermediate stations. The branch was a stronghold of the renowned MGW 2-4-0s (now class G2), almost the only Midland design about which the strongly G&SW-minded locomotive hierarchy of the Great Southern could find a good word to say. On 3 December 1960 one of the survivors is No 655 (once *Clonsilla*) of 1897, on the 13.00, not seriously exercised on a line with a 25 mph limit and 40 minutes allowed for the 9½ miles.

Here is 655 on arrival at Ballaghaderreen, about to retire to the shed, to doze the afternoon away until called upon to work the 08.00 next morning.

The same engine outside Ballaghaderreen's locomotive depot, on 8 June 1961. No 655 was one of the class rebuilt with two different types of superheated boiler, first Belpaire and subsequently the round-topped version seen here. Her bedraggled appearance belies the achievements of these engines in relatively recent years on the Sligo line, until the advent of the diesel locomotives in the late 1950s. Not a soul is to be seen, not unusual perhaps – but surprising as this was the day of the visit by the grand railtour of June 1961.

On a glacial February day in 1963 an ex-Midland 'J18', No 574, is the branch engine, about to leave the terminus on the 11.50 to Kilfree…

…and pause at Edmondstown's rural station. No 574 is one of a couple of similar engines endowed with a 'modern' cab, so designed that the corner of the roof threatened the drivers' heads, and therefore having had its cut-out plated in to give the ugly effect seen here.

115

Ballaghaderreen lost its trains later in 1963, leaving Loughrea as the only survivor of the twelve termini of branches off the MGW's main lines to Galway, Westport and Sligo. Indeed, the Loughrea line ended its days with a diesel locomotive hauled service as late as 1975. Here however it is No 583, a 'J18', heading the train at Attymon Junction in October 1962, while the connecting Up Day Mail from Galway waits at the main-line platform. It's the second, and last, train of the day, arriving at Loughrea at 17.00

The branch train here in June 1961 has a typical makeup: a 19th-century six-wheel third brake, a 1950s 'tin van' and a corridor bogie. The train pauses at Dunsandle, the single stop on the line, and the engine is the usual Midland 0-6-0, 'J19' No 610 of 1888.

No 583 runs round her train on arrival at Loughrea. In the background is the two-road engine shed, water tower, and turntable – usual provision for a branch-line terminus, if generous in relation to the number of trains!

The Limerick–Foynes line still had a passenger service of sorts, the one daily 'mixed' taking just over 2½ hours over the 27-mile journey if punctual. I cannot think that many passengers undertook this voyage – certainly not on 25 November 1961, when 'J15' 164, though not challenged by the schedule, finally decanted us at Limerick platform at 19.20 after spending twenty minutes shunting outside the station. Here she stands outside the Foynes loco shed with her train. I now regret not taking more interest in Irish coaching stock; the accommodation here looks like a G&SW six-wheeler ex-first/second composite, though I don't recall travelling in particular comfort.

Wexford and Waterford steam sheds remained open to the end, and were often called upon to provide power when diesels were unavailable. The sparse local service from Wexford to Rosslare was often so substituted. Unrebuilt 'J15' 187 of 1882, looking as close as possible to her as-built condition with an original archaic tender, has brought a morning train from Rosslare Harbour into Wexford (North) on 11 November 1961.

The former D&SE's North Wexford line still had a couple of trains each way, nominally railcar-worked but in practice often steam-substituted. On 28 October 1961, 'J15' No 125 has the 16.25 Macmine Junction–Waterford, speeding down the 1 in 60 of Ballyanne bank at the site of the famous incident described on p85. The trees conceal the fact that the train consists only of a single coach, plus two vans! In D&SER days, and into the GSR era, the Mail carried a restaurant car portion for Waterford, reversing at Macmine Junction and running over the North Wexford line – hard to credit now.

After the bottom of the bank, the line turned westwards, through Mount Elliott tunnel and over the five-span opening Barrow Bridge, seen with No 125 and train crossing in the evening light.

NCC Lines:
The Black North

'Black' only in the colour of its locomotives: the former Northern Counties section of the UTA was a remarkably smartly-operated system – what was left of it, after the closure of all but the Derry, Portrush and Larne lines – manned by efficient and genial staff, particularly the enginemen. Visits to the NCC usually happened in summer, when steam was in full cry. In winter apart from Larne line locals, frequently steam-worked in replacement of doubtfully-reliable railcars, there were few attractions, and at any time the limited motive power diet of 'Jeep' tanks and 'Moguls' made recording the often exciting running a more profitable experience than photography. Some of the photos which follow were taken in 1964/5, on holiday visits to Ulster.

The spirit of the NCC is well caught in this scene. The occasion is the final day of the grand Irish railtour of 3–10 June 1961, the engine is the last NCC 4-4-0, the now-preserved 'Castle' No 74 *Dunluce Castle*, and the crew are Driver Jimmy Keenan and Fireman Simpson. The engine, properly cleaned up for the occasion, has just done a final 62 mph down the bank to Antrim. The lined UTA livery shows up well, as does the numberplate (be it noted, brass plates were still used on the 'Jeeps' in the 1950s) with its unusual figure '7'. This is not an economical inverted '2', but a form occasionally seen in Ulster and Scotland. The Manson tablet catcher was effective at speed though not infallible, particularly on a rough-riding engine.

Belfast's York Road station was hardly an architectural gem, if only because of the destructive blitz of April and May 1941 and subsequent uninspired rebuilding. 'Jeep' 8 is heading the 17.30 to Larne Harbour in July 1965, with steam still active in summer on front-line duties. Mail is being loaded into one of the three vans at the front of the train. Invisible but in charge of No 8 is Alan Robinson, even at that late date extracting some memorable performances from a deteriorating stud of locomotives.

The completion in 1934 of the flying junction at Bleach Green, 4½ miles from York Road, eliminated the need for main-line trains to reverse at Greenisland, and doubtless led ultimately to the demise of the GNR line to Derry, no longer competitive. An unidentified 'Jeep' swings over the viaduct on an up express, with the Knockagh escarpment and Antrim War Memorial in the background. On the left is Bleach Green platform on the down Larne line. To cross the viaduct at 70 mph and reach a quick 80 only three miles or so from the terminus was one of the excitements of travel on the NCC, and perhaps in those years this was the spot in Ireland where such a speed was most likely to be achieved.

Ballyclare Junction station, at the top of the climb on the 'new' line from sea level at Belfast, was closed in 1961 (look at the footbridge!). The branch to Ballyclare went off almost a mile further down the line, at Kingsbog, itself the summit of the much longer but less steep ascent from Antrim. No 52 heads a down Portrush train.

Heavy trains were often piloted from Belfast up the 1 in 76 climb to Ballyclare Junction, the 08.35 summer Saturday express to Derry and Portrush being one such, usually loading to 10 coaches and a van or two, perhaps 340 tons – quite enough for the usual 'Jeep'. The pilot would come off at Kingsbog and run on to the stub of the closed Ballyclare branch, retained for the purpose. This manoeuvre exemplified the NCC's typically slick working, the stop perhaps lasting little over a minute. Here, on 29 August 1964, Driver Bell on No 9 is on the move after 86 seconds, Mitchell on No 6 (the pilot) having already got the road for his return light to Belfast. On 5 August 1961 Lettman and Magill took 62 seconds, and on 27 July 1963, Steenson put the pilot off and was moving forward again in just under a minute. How different from the proceedings at Shap Summit!

No 6 brings a down train into Coleraine in August 1965. She had emerged from overhaul two months earlier, but the unshaded numerals on the front bufferbeam suggest that the rundown has started,

and Nos 7 and 8 were never to run again after that year. Note all four coaches (apart from the buffet car) of the splendid York Road-built 1934/5 'North Atlantic' set, at the head of the 10-coach train. It is said that the wide windows were intended to be identical with those currently used on the LMS, but were made six inches wider in error! The 1938 colour-light resignalling at Coleraine was in part the responsibility of OS Nock, whose professional visits facilitated his Irish travelling and recording.

The Derry line crossed the lower Bann shortly after leaving Coleraine. The lifting bridge seen here dates from 1924, on a site downstream from the original viaduct, requiring a diversion of the main line. A short length of the old line was retained, leading to the harbour branch, then still busy with coastal shipping but latterly disused and closed in 1966. A Derry-bound train crosses on 29 July 1962.

A common sight at Portrush on a summer weekend, when engines from down excursion traffic would run to Coleraine and back for servicing, coupled in procession to reduce congestion on the single line. As many as six together were not unknown, but No 6 leads a crocodile of only three, returning past Dhu Varren, just outside Portrush.

The classic view of Portrush, with the station full of stock for return excursions. On Sunday, 6 August 1961, Driver Jim Simpson with No 3 is about to lift the nine-coach 19.05 to Belfast away up that nasty 1 in 76 start, almost from the platform end. Possibly they will be helped by some of the sand blown from the beach below the lineside, which periodically needed to be cleared from the tracks.

Four years later, on 24 July 1965, a grimy No 52 is at grips with the gradient. She will be followed by No 8 (to be withdrawn two months later) on the Saturday 19.30 up. Whatever her condition, no complaint could be made about her performance on the eleven-mile grind from Antrim start up to Kingsbog with ten coaches, without falling below 42 mph. This was done, according to driver Jim Coulter of Coleraine, on 30% cutoff with the main valve of the regulator just open, and he rounded off the run with a brisk 80 mph at Whitehouse. The previous year Driver Heffron had done better, with No 3 and ten coaches (320 tons), averaging just over 50 mph from Templepatrick to Kingsbog with no speed lower than 48 on the 1 in No 186. The presence of an excursion from Dublin in 'black-and-tan' livery, and headed by a GM diesel, is a sign of the times.

The Apprentice Boys' annual celebrations at Derry involved a good deal of extra traffic. Here a special passes Downhill on 11 August 1962 behind No 5, at perhaps the most spectacular location on the NCC system, with the (atheist) Bishop of Derry's Mussenden Temple on the clifftop in the background. The photo reveals that there were still some ancient straight-sided bogie coaches in existence – presumably thought good enough for special traffic of this nature. They were, I think, 48 ft long and cannot have weighed much over 20 tons apiece. In 1960 I rode (in a Lisburn local!) in one of a set of eight, which with a van had a total tare of only 180 tons.

Accommodation at (London)derry Waterside was limited, but visiting locomotives on such busy days could be parked and watered on the siding alongside the station, just behind the shed.

The Larne line survived, and still survives, with a suburban service which included a surprising number of short workings on a line itself of only 24 miles. Some terminated, as here, at Carrickfergus. On 23 July 1965 the station looks shabby, but unlike most other examples of Berkeley Deane Wise's characterful architecture it has now been fully restored. This too is a typical NCC scene, inasmuch as RM (Mac) Arnold, the indefatigable chronicler of NCC affairs, is on the platform talking to the fireman while Driver Davis runs round his train with No 4 before working the 18.03 back to York Road.

In 1925 the NCC opened four halts close to Carrickfergus – the station is visible only a quarter-mile off in the background of this shot of No 9 passing Clipperstown with a boat train from Larne.

Downshire Park was another halt a mile the other side of Carrickfergus, with similarly basic, if rather better maintained, accommodation. The waters of Belfast Lough wash the wall at the left. No 4 passes on a ballast working in August 1964.

More work on the line; No 52 and crew doze during some leisurely Sunday morning unloading of new sleepers beside the 'White Harbour', just before the tunnel beneath White Head, leading to Whitehead itself a mile further on. The tunnel was on the down line only; when the section was doubled in 1929, the up road used a cutting closer to the sea.

Whitehead was very much the creation of the Belfast and Northern Counties Railway, which put much effort into both residential and tourist development – fulfilling, as JRL Currie writes, "many of the functions of a local authority". These included construction of a promenade and landing stage, bandstand and famously, the spectacular Gobbins and Black Head paths; and 'Villa Tickets' were issued to residents. The tourist trade led to the opening in 1907 of the excursion station, to the eventual benefit of the Railway Preservation Society of Ireland whose headquarters it now forms. In this 1965 photo a tired-looking No 5 heads an up train, with two North Atlantic coaches at the front.

At the other end of Whitehead station on 3 August 1962, No 5 waits with a heavy (8 bogies and a van) evening train for Larne Harbour. Up the hill on the right lies Edward Road, at the top of which Mac Arnold lived, within easy hearing distance, if not quite sight, of the railway he loved.

A Winter's Tale:
The Beet Season

The winter offered fewer possibilities to the steam enthusiast for travel, but opened up photo-opportunities for the car-owner – for the months from October to February were those of the Beet Campaign. The Irish Sugar Company, a 'semi-State' concern like CIÉ, had four factories, all rail-served, and sugar beet was a major agricultural product. It was essential to maintain a consistent flow of beet while keeping pace with production; so the supply of empty wagons to loading points, hauling full trains to the factories and returning the empties, required careful organisation. Before me is CIÉ's weekly circular for the first week of October 1962, in itself an interesting period piece, announcing the imminent start of the campaign with appropriate exhortations to staff: "Supply of Coal Trucks for Beet… laden open [coal] trucks on hands will when empty, be deemed to be available for beet unless specific authority is to the contrary..." "On the promptness and accuracy of the advice to the Inspector at the factory… will depend the board's ability to deal with the considerable traffics offering other than Beet…", and so on.

The circular does indeed deal with many other matters than beet. Railborne livestock traffic might have been declining, but specials were required every day for various fairs, and it is salutary for instance to read that on the Friday, 120 wagons were to be supplied in advance to Ballinasloe at the end of the week's fair, over and above the previous 100. As for Monday's special from Ballybrophy for Listowel races, it is good to know that "this Special should make a good run and every effort made to expedite it…" (the engine being needed elsewhere), and the following day racegoers from Dublin had the unusual treat of a buffet-car special running over the North Kerry line.

Four months' work shifting beet, on top of normal requirements, needed a good many extra engines, meaning steam, and the main burden was shared between the 0-6-0s of the old companies – typically GS&WR 'J15's and their MGW equivalents, 'J18/19's. A complex timetable was established; trains were identified by number, with appropriate prefixes for the factories – BC for Carlow, BM Mallow, BS Thurles and BT Tuam. Empties from the factories were given even numbers, and vice-versa. Additional overload trains could be necessary, and punctuality was not always immaculate. This was one problem for the photographer, in addition to the short daylight hours (and much of the traffic moved by night) and questionable weather – but there were many locations where steam was unlikely to appear under any other circumstances.

Perhaps this shot encapsulates the beet season. Saturday, 21 October 1961, a wet day in the west of Ireland: the farmer stops heaving beet into a wagon, to hold his horse's head while an old Midland engine rattles by with a long train of empties. The engine is a 'J18', No 592; the location is Belleville siding, between Ballyglunin and Athenry; the train is BT70, 13.05 from Tuam factory sidings with empties for return loads from stations to Portarlington, arrival there at 01.40 next morning. One trusts the crew will be relieved en route. The engine will run on to stable at Kildare.

At the other end of the country, a shot for the record, if not one to dwell on. *Macha* was not long for this world when photographed in October 1961, reduced to shuffling wagons of beet at Kilbarry sidings, at the north end of Cork tunnel: perhaps an indication of the shortage of motive power in the beet season. She must have had a few miles still to work out after a brief moment in the limelight in the summer, on the grand joint railtour of Ireland.

A better October day and a more cheerful scene on the outskirts of Cork. 'J9' No 250 wheels empties from Mallow past Tivoli, two miles beyond Cork, for beet from stations to Killeagh on the Youghal line.

Beet specials to Carlow factory were perhaps the most accessible, and more often ran in daylight. BC35 from Kildare took a scheduled five hours over the 26 miles – allowing for 'as required' visits to Kilberry and Grangemellon sidings and (on Tuesdays and Fridays) a trip up the Ballylinan branch. The latter was accessed by crossing the Barrow river at Athy, over the reinforced-concrete bridge built when the branch was opened to the Wolfhill collieries in 1918 – by which time its raison d' etre, the wartime coal shortage, was almost ended. The branch never had a passenger service and was soon cut back to Ballylinan and restricted to beet traffic. In October 1960 'J15' No 149 crosses the river, with a couple of wagons at the head of the train for the asbestos factory on the west bank.

Ballylinan terminus was no more than a siding in a field, reached after running through several other fields and across some rural level crossings. The lamp at Lanigan Lane was probably last lit some time ago, and seems to have been used for target practice. Old No 149 waits for the guard to open the gates.

Another line, finally closed in 1963 as was the Ballylinan branch, was 'Motte's Line', the financially disastrous 24-mile connection from Muine Bheag (Bagenalstown) on the GS&W to Palace East on the D&SE. Originally envisaged as a trunk route, it soon degenerated into the rustic condition we shall see, carrying, however, significant beet traffic for Carlow. The small loco shed at Bagenalstown was reopened for the season, with crews who were prepared to lodge provided from Dublin and elsewhere. 'J15' No 172 runs into Bagenalstown with empties in October 1961, where the relief men are waiting.

The first station on the line, with 172 passing, was Goresbridge where those seats on the short platform would have been last used by passengers in 1931. The line's restriction to 25 mph gave a pursuing vehicle on the rural road system a fair chance, and the scenery made it an attractive destination for photography.

Here on 28 October 1961 is another 'J15', No 197, at Borris, 74 miles from Kingsbridge, as indicated by the characteristic GS&W granite milepost. No 197 is working an empty train, but has come off to do some shunting of loaded wagons, to be picked up on the return.

Construction of the 15-arch viaduct at Borris no doubt swallowed most of the capital of the original company. No 197 has collected her train and crosses on the way to Ballywilliam and Palace East.

The goat seems untroubled by the hurried arrival of a black van, closely followed by the passage of 197, whose crew are clearly entering into the spirit of things. The white disc on the tender denotes an oil-burning locomotive (from the days of fuel problems, at their worst immediately after 1945) – indicating to signalmen that a passing engine would not need to stop in the section to 'bale out', ie clean the fire, only too frequent a happening in the time of the 'duff'. No 197 was not in fact one of those converted in 1947, but had been the subject of a further oil burner trial as late as 1954. The white disc was accordingly unnecessary; it can just be seen that some joker at Inchicore had painted it with a clock face!

Here 197 is passing Ballyling, a remote siding under Mount Leinster still producing an occasional wagon of beet. Some readers may remember pausing there in 1960 or 1963 on one of the railtours of the period. Years later my wife and I found the crossing-keeper's cottage still inhabited by the two elderly ladies who were happy to recall the sociable evenings spent with the 'lads from Bagenalstown', working beet specials unhurriedly through the night.

And lastly the same engine is panting up the final mile of the climb to Palace East, where the D&SERs North Wexford line runs alongside the GS&WR branch.

On 28 October 1961 BC35 leaves the Cork line at Cherryville Junction behind 'J15' No 132, on a day memorable for more than the fine weather. The train, 32 wagons and van, includes some general traffic as well as beet for Carlow, shunting being needed at most stops.

No 132 (not to be confused with the Great Northern engine of the same number; on paper, but not on the locomotives, an 'N' was added to the GN numbers) stands at Kildangan's tiny station, where two members of the van party were invited to join Driver Bowe and Fireman Dowling of Inchicore. No 132 was one of the very few GSR/CIÉ engines to retain the double handle fitting on the smokebox door, doubtless easier to tighten but presumably more liable to slack off in running. This type had been generally used when the double doors of the early period were replaced during the 1920s and 1930s, but was soon altered to the familiar locking handwheel. Oddly enough the 800 class were given the two-handle version from new in 1939/40, only to have it changed later.

At the next stop, Kilberry siding, three wagons were put off for the peat moss traffic from the adjoining bog, served by its own 2ft gauge railway. The footplate party changed over, and for the first time I found myself handling the regulator of a steam locomotive, not a difficult task in view of 132's easy mastery of the load, but stopping an unbraked train at the water column at Athy (seen here) was another matter entirely, even under instruction. I suppose it was better to have stopped three or four yards short than to have overshot and needed to reverse, quite hard work on a 'J15' with an awkward handwheel, as David Houston and I were to discover on a later trip with Joe Bowe. The cab of a 'J15' offered few comforts, but the controls were otherwise handy enough. The firedoor was the convenient sliding type, by no means universal but adopted, for instance on such latter-day types as the LMS 'Duchesses', no less. On the Irish engines the handle was within easy reach of the driver, so that the old practice, of the latter handing the door for every shovelful without needing to take his eyes from the road, was generally followed.

143

Plenty of unrebuilt 'J15's survived to share the load of the beet campaign. No 253 of the last-built (1903) batch of 'J15's was turned out on a damp November day in 1960 to work the 09.40 goods from Waterford to Mallow, an 8 hour, 75 mile trip regularly rostered for steam during the beet season. Carroll's Cross, between Waterford and Dungarvan, has a couple of wagons of beet ready for someone else to pick up. This line survived until 1967, technically in the ownership (as far as Fermoy) of the Fishguard and Rosslare Railways and Harbours Company (F&RR&HC). This was the route of the 'Rosslare Express,' the boat train to Cork equipped when new in 1907 with the finest rolling stock in Ireland.

Kilmacthomas is, or was, the next station. No 253 is shunting a van off here, perhaps for Flavin's (more accurately Flahavan's) Mill siding. The mill was established about 1785; still in the same family ownership, its Organic Oats won a Healthy Eating award in 2016…

…but alas, since 1967 can no longer be taken away on the viaduct over the Mahon river which once powered the mill.

No 253 takes refreshment at Cappoquin. She has a relatively modern, probably 3345 gallon, tender, useful on such a long run. The Blackwater river is tidal up to Cappoquin, and the G&SWR at one time issued circular excursion tickets, Cork to Cappoquin by rail via Mallow, thence by paddle steamer to Youghal, and back to Cork by rail.

As the shadows lengthen 253 leaves Cappoquin over the Blackwater viaduct. At this point the photographic party started to think about the night's lodging. Cappoquin was not far from Mount Melleray, the Cistercian monastery reputed to offer hospitality to travellers, as indeed it proved that night, even to three students from godless Trinity College.

The elegant locomotives of the Waterford, Limerick & Western Railway had all disappeared by the 1960s, and that long and lonely 'main' line from Waterford to Sligo was operated, if by steam, with former G&SW and MGW engines, usually on the southern and northern sections of the line respectively. On this afternoon in October 1961 however, it was a real stranger, one of the highly-regarded pair of ex-D&SER 2-6-0s (GSR Class K2), No 461, working from Thurles via Clonmel to Waterford with BS48, both beet empties and ordinary wagonload traffic. She is shunting one of the latter off at Grange, the last station before Waterford.

And then 461 crosses the (Kilkenny) River Blackwater bridge, shortly before the junction with the GS&W line from Kilkenny at Dunkitt.

The 'Southern Railway of Ireland' was an ill-fated concern, falling permanently into receivership even before completion and being worked by the WL&WR. Nevertheless its line provided a tolerably direct connection from the prosperous town of Clonmel to Dublin via Thurles, with through coaches in its latter days, and was perhaps unfortunate to fall victim to the closure programme of 1963. Its daily goods train remained steam-hauled, and it gave useful access to Thurles beet factory in season. 'J9' No 251 has just left Clonmel with a beet extra for Thurles in November 1961, and is passing the grass-grown but still used Powerstown Park platform serving the adjacent racecourse. In the right background, Clonmel's surprisingly consequential loco shed and water tower are just visible beyond the field to the right of the picture.

No 251 and her train are caught here in a rural moment just north of Clonmel.

Fethard was the only place of any importance on the Clonmel–Thurles line. Rebuilt 'J15' No 179 is in charge of a Thurles-bound livestock special in September 1962.

No 253 has the morning goods from Thurles to Clonmel on 14 October 1961, pausing at Laffan's Bridge to cross the up passenger service and do some shunting. What can be the contents of all those wicker-covered carboys?

Half an hour earlier, 253 had been entering the loop at Horse and Jockey; the photo is taken from the bridge carrying the main road from Dublin to Cork, then a narrow humped stone arch and now replaced by motorway!

On the former D&SER's North Wexford line again, we follow BT40, empties at 03.10 from Carlow to Wexford via Palace East, and fortunately running late on 11 November 1961. A very early start from Dublin was involved, and the journey included a puncture. No need to waste time with the jack, when three passengers were available to lift and support one corner of the van… It looks as if no wagons can be left here, at Chapel Halt, until those at the loading bank and fouling the loop are cleared. The engine is the usual 'J15', No 172.

No 172 is running down past Sparrowsland siding, at the top of the steep descent to Macmine Junction – the siding was still nominally open for beet traffic, but evidently not much used!

Macmine is/was picturesquely situated beside the River Slaney, just in view on the right. The junction with the D&SE main line from Dublin to Wexford is hidden by the wagons of 172's train. Macmine can scarcely have generated much traffic, but once had moments of serious activity, as when the Down Mail divided here into Wexford and Waterford portions, the latter reversing and climbing away towards Palace East.

After the challenging negotiation of 'Motte's Line' and the tricky descent from Palace East (480ft above sea level), crews of loose-coupled trains must have found the last few miles after Killurin along the banks of the tidal Slaney into Wexford a welcome change. No 172 with her remaining handful of wagons nears the end of her journey.

In Wexford itself, trains must contend with road traffic along the quays. Still on 11 November 1961, No 111 ('The Sergeant') has the midday goods for Rosslare…

…and negotiates her own short-sea passage before leaving Wexford.

Rosslare Strand, over three miles from the Harbour station, was the junction with the F&RR&HC's South Wexford line, on to which the goods has been shunted for the mid-morning passenger from Dublin to pass.

A relaxed Saturday afternoon on the short branch to Waterford South. This had until 1906 been the terminus of the line from Dungarvan and ultimately Mallow, but in that year the F&RR&HC completed its route from Mallow by crossing the River Suir and entering Waterford's main station on the north bank, the South branch becoming a short spur from Grace Dieu Junction, a half-mile short of the Suir Bridge. Passenger services ceased in 1908 but the branch was kept, latterly to serve Irish Ironfounders premises on the station site. On 4 November 1961 unrebuilt No 116 is rolling a few wagons cautiously down the branch. She has acquired a modern tender, one of those built for the 342 class 4-4-0s in 1936.

A view of 116 amid the remains of Waterford South, looking across the Suir with Waterford locomotive depot prominent opposite. Waterford (North) station itself is barely distinguishable in the distance on the far bank, close to the road bridge leading to the city.

A reminder that after the division of the Great Northern, that company's locomotives found work elsewhere on the CIÉ system. 'SG2' No 181 is working a load of gypsum from Kingscourt over the MGW line south of Navan, in January 1961. No regular passengers had changed at Kilmessan for Athboy, or indeed alighted at all, since 1947. However it is not the first time GN engines had used the line. When the Tolka bridge on the main line outside Amiens Street was destroyed by flooding in 1954, passenger services were turned round at Clontarf, but goods for Dublin was worked from Drogheda via the GN line to Navan, reversing there on to the MGW's Meath branch, and GN power was employed throughout.

No 181 and her train have just joined the MGW main line on what, after the singling of most of the main line in the '30s, was its only double-track section, at Clonsilla.

The end of the line, in every sense. I never travelled on the Cork, Bandon & South Coast (CB&SC) system except at the very end, on the last steam-hauled passenger train, the IRRS special on St Patrick's Day 1961, worked by 'Bandon Tank' No 464, one of the line's well-liked 4-6-0Ts. At the end of the outward trip she faces the Atlantic: Baltimore may not quite have been Europe's farthest-west railhead, but due westward the next railway was an isolated Inuit-operated line in the interior of Labrador. The CB&SC closed two weeks later.

ACKNOWLEDGEMENTS AND BIBLIOGRAPHY

Personal experience and recollection can only go so far: much of the historical, geographical and technical information in this book comes from the sources given below, and I am glad to acknowledge the debt I owe to their authors, and for the pleasure their writings have given – but I cannot evade responsibility for any errors of fact herein. The book could hardly have happened without the friendship of those mentioned in the text, which has also benefitted from the editorial suggestions of my wife Georgina. Thanks go also to Malcolm Johnston and the team at Colourpoint for their work on the text, and in particular for the results achieved from the original colour slides, which have had a hard life over the past half-century.

Arnold, RM: *Steam over Belfast Lough,* Oakwood Press, Lingfield (1969)

Arnold, RM: *NCC Saga,* David & Charles, Newton Abbot (1973)

Clements, J & McMahon, M: *Locomotives of the GSR,* Colourpoint, Newtownards (2008)

Clements, RN & Robbins, JM: *ABC of Irish Locomotives,* Ian Allan Ltd, Shepperton (1949, facsimile ed 2000)

Coakham, D: *Irish Broad Gauge Carriages,* Midland Publishing Ltd, Hinckley (2004)

Crockart, A & Patience, J: *Rails Around Belfast,* Midland Publishing Ltd, Hinckley (2004)

Currie, JRL: *The Northern Counties Railway,* vol 2, David & Charles, Newton Abbot (1974)

Johnson, S: *Johnson's Atlas and Gazetteer of the Railways of Ireland,* Midland Publishing Ltd, Earl Shilton (1997)

Johnston, N: *Locomotives of the GNR(I),* Colourpoint, Newtownards (1999)

Liddle, L: *From Connemara to Cock o' the North,* Colourpoint, Newtownards (2002)

Liddle, L: *Steam Finale,* Irish Railway Record Society, London (1964)

Murray, KA & McNeill, DB: *The Great Southern and Western Railway,* Irish Railway Record Society, Dublin (1976)

Patterson, EM: *The Great Northern Railway (Ireland),* 2nd ed, Oakwood Press, Usk (2003)

Pender, B & Richards, H: *Irish Railways Today,* Transport Research Associates, Dublin (1976)

Pryce, I & McAllister, L (eds): *Steaming in Three Centuries,* Irish Railway Record Society, London (2006)

Scott, WT: *Locomotives of the LMS NCC and its Predecessors,* Colourpoint, Newtownards (2008)

Shepherd, WE: *The Dublin & South Eastern Railway,* David & Charles, Newton Abbot (1974)

Shepherd, WE: *The Midland Great Western Railway of Ireland,* Midland Publishing Ltd, Earl Shilton (1994)

Also:

Working timetables and circulars of CIÉ, UTA and GNR(I)

The Railway Magazine (various issues)

Journal of the Irish Railway Record Society (various numbers)